Tips & Tactics for

Serving Customers *on the* Internet

by Joanne Y. Cleaver

Inc. Business Resources
Boston, Massachusetts

Published by *Inc.* Business Resources,
a division of Gruner + Jahr USA Publishing,
publisher of *Inc.* magazine.
Copyright © 2001 by Gruner + Jahr USA Publishing,
Boston, MA. All rights reserved.

Editorial Director: Bradford W. Ketchum, Jr.
Book Project Manager: Gail E. Anderson
Text Designer: Martha Abdella

This publication is designed to provide accurate and
authoritative information in regard to the subject matter
covered. However, the publisher is not engaged in rendering
legal, accounting, or other professional advice. If legal
advice or other expert assistance is required, the services
of a competent professional should be sought. Companies that
conduct e-commerce on the Internet are evolving constantly,
as are URLs. While every effort has been made to ensure the
accuracy of information in this book, readers should be aware
that Web addresses are subject to change.

This book may be purchased in bulk at discounted rates for
sales promotions, premiums, or fund-raising. Custom books
and excerpts of this publication are available. Contact:
Custom Publishing Sales Dept.,
Inc. Business Resources, 38 Commercial Wharf,
Boston, MA 02110-3883 (1-800-394-1746).

About the author: Joanne Y. Cleaver has been writing about
small-business marketing and operations since 1981, and
about e-commerce and Internet business trends since 1993.
A frequent contributor to regional and national business
publications, she is a graduate of Northwestern University,
with a master's degree in journalism.

ISBN 1-58230-016-X

First Edition

Printed in the United States of America.

www.inc.com

Contents

Chapter 1   **5**

Supporting Online Customers

- E-commerce gives "service" a whole new meaning
- Addressing the top 10 complaints from online consumers
- How to detect—and eliminate—service bottlenecks
- Tracking customer questions and applying real-time response

Chapter 2   **17**

E-mail: Why It's the Universal Tool

- First step to online service: capitalize on e-mail's key functions
- What type of response do *your* customers expect?
- Tracking e-mail in today's electronic frenzy
- Provide insider contact—and post your address everywhere
- Managing e-mail databases means cleaning house regularly

Chapter 3   **26**

Database-driven E-mail

- Building your database—and using it to target customers
- Eight ways to make an e-mail newsletter click
- E-mail service providers: sizing up options for outsourcing
- Using "opt-in" tactics to maximize e-mail response

Chapter 4   **43**

Enriched Site Content

- What constitutes "rich" content?
- How to leverage the friendly FAQ format
- Betting on bulletin boards and real-time chats
- Links to useful sites spell added customer service

Contents

Chapter 5   **58**

Real-time Contact
- Where traditional technology (e.g., toll-free phone lines) fits in
- Making the most of instant messaging, chats, and voice-over-Internet
- Training your customer support staff

Chapter 6   **72**

Fulfillment: Betting on the Back Office
- E-commerce software packages integrate fulfillment functions
- In-house vs. outsource: weighing the pros and cons

Chapter 7   **79**

Tracking the Return
- A dozen key indicators for measuring online results
- Going beyond simple return on investment

CRM Technology Matrix   **92**
Summary chart shows what hardware and software you need to implement online customer relationship management (CRM) functions, including e-mail communications, service support, and inventory control

CyberSpeak   **94**
A glossary of terms for clicking with the Internet

Online CRM Resources   **96**
A guide to the Web sites of hardware, software, and service companies that offer customer relationship management tools

Chapter 1

Supporting Online Customers

Customers contacting Advantage Credit International, of Pensacola, Fla., aren't in the mood to wait long for answers: They're mortgage officers trying to get details about the creditworthiness of consumers applying for home mortgages. CEO Timothy Handley expects them to get a summary of their applicants' credit status within 30 seconds of submitting their requests through his Web site. Most of the reports are computer-generated "credit scores" for customers who need to pinpoint specific glitches and straighten out misrepresented information. Advantage provides handcrafted reports explained either online or over the phone by one of its credit analysts.

Handley's blend of automation and personalized service has made Advantage Credit a must for mortgage brokers and their anxious clients who know they can count on an immediate turnaround backed up by expert advice. His commitment to service has helped propel the company to $9 million in sales—and has garnered customer loyalty in the process. The moral of the story: Attracting customers to your Web site is one thing. Winning sales from them, retaining their loyalty, and developing an ongoing, profitable relationship with them is quite another.

Customers who buy through your Web site have high expectations. They expect the same kind of service they would get if they were in your store or office. They crave one-on-one reassurance, and they expect you to treat them as efficiently and courteously as the leading online pros. In fact, they expect you to be more nimble because you are online.

It's important, however, not to overestimate the role of the Internet in serving customers. Customer relationship management (CRM) is not a linear process with a clearly defined beginning, middle, and end. "In the virtual world, you don't have the confidence of seeing a person," says Rob

Support

Niederman, director of e-business consulting for Alternative Resources Corp., a technology consulting firm in Barrington, Ill. "The sequence of events is literally different than a person-to-person transaction."

Since customers' questions and expectations are as individual as they are, it's impossible to create a software program that completely automates every touchpoint. And customers don't want that, anyway. They want software and information that lets them connect with your employees, so that their questions and problems can be addressed personally.

Not your father's customer service. In the late 1990s, e-commerce proponents believed that all customer functions could be automated through the Internet. Their ideal was to eliminate all personal contact between customers and companies. However, customers rejected that philosophy. Customers will tolerate some "hands-off" functions, but they do not want to feel as if you are using technology to keep them at arm's length. The more important a transaction or communication is to them, the more likely they are to insist on personal contact before buying. This is especially true if the purchase is expensive, involves a complicated product or service, is emotionally significant, or is the customer's first time buying from your company.

Dynamic relationships. A great advantage of online customer service is that the feedback loop is dramatically shortened. You no longer have to print a catalog and then wait for customers to ask questions, order, return, and comment, before learning what products are most appealing and why. And customers' expectations can be met dynamically through various Internet tools—even software that can tell your customers when you are sold out of a particular item, that can count down the last of those items, that can flag your staff for reordering, and then post a note on your site indicating when the item will be back in stock. Furthermore, you can capture the potential sale by programming your site so that a box pops up offering customers the chance to be automatically notified by e-mail when the desired item is available.

You can anticipate customers' questions by continually posting updated information about your products and services on your site. If you find that customers read your descriptions of air conditioner parts but continually call to ask the same questions, you don't have to wait until the next edition of the catalog to change the description online.

Up-front expectations. Customers generally define "service" on the Internet the same way they do in the brick-and-mortar world, with one exception: They want it faster. The Internet's culture of immediate gratification sets a high bar for e-commerce sites.

Unspoken expectations. Customers know that when they communicate with you or buy through your Web site, they're cutting out many tedious steps for you as well as themselves. Instead of talking to a service rep over the phone and waiting as he or she enters information, customers are typing that same information directly into your computers. They can see the approval of their credit card happen (or not) before their eyes. Much of your process is transparent to them. That's good,

TIP Voice-over-Internet protocol (VoIP), an emerging, technology that enables customer service reps to actually speak through a customer's computer (via its speakers) while that customer is online at the site may be disorienting and distracting for some customers. So, be sure to gauge your customers' enthusiasm for being technological guinea pigs before inflicting cutting-edge technology on them. They're much more likely to appreciate simple, easy-to-use, responsive customer service tools than gee-whiz technology that doesn't really serve them.

Support

because they feel more closely connected with your company when they're actively engaged in the ordering process. Conversely, if your site is studded with technical complications such as confusing product information, ignored e-mail requests, and broken links, customers will be inclined to buy elsewhere on the Web, from a company that appears to have its e-commerce act together.

Once the customer hits the "Send" button, it's up to you to provide smooth follow-up. This fulfills the unspoken—but reasonable—expectation of the customer that you're upholding your end of the bargain. A steady stream of confirmations, says Alternate Resources' Niederman, brings back some of the comforts of nonverbal communication. "Customers believe that ordering through e-commerce is faster and more accurate than other methods," he adds. "They appreciate the high-tech convenience, but they crave high-touch service even more."

Behind the curve. Resource Marketing, a Columbus, Ohio, Internet marketing firm, tracked the success of online sales during the holiday 1999 selling season by purchasing from 50 Web sites. What it found was positively "Grinchly." Twenty percent of the packages that reps from Resource Marketing ordered arrived late or never; 25% of the time the shoppers weren't even able to place orders, due to technical glitches; and 36% of the sites had busy or unhelpful customer service numbers.

Kelly Mooney, managing director of intelligence at Resource Marketing, says that the message is loud and clear: The customers need immediate help at the point of transaction. If they don't get it, they will probably abandon their shopping carts, or never return to that site again. And if they do return, the online shopping site had better be able to recognize them, and customer service reps had better be able to tap into that customer's entire data file— from prior purchases to the addresses of gift recipients.

Detecting service bottlenecks. To discover if customers are getting hung

TOP 10 COMPLAINTS FROM ONLINE CONSUMERS

Accenture (formerly Andersen Consulting), which includes e-commerce among its specialties, conducted a survey of consumers who tried to shop online during the 1999 end-of-year holiday season. While the shoppers ranked their Internet experiences as better than their experiences with traditional stores and mail-order catalogs, more than a third who ran into glitches at a site simply surfed away and shopped elsewhere.

According to the Accenture survey, at least six of customers' top 10 complaints derive from poor customer service.

Complaint	Percent of Internet Buyers
1. Item was out of stock	64%
2. Product was not delivered on time	40%
3. Paid too much for delivery	38%
4. Connection or download trouble	36%
5. Didn't receive confirmation or status report on purchase	28%
6. Selections were limited	27%
7. Web site was too difficult to navigate	26%
8. Web site didn't provide information needed to make purchase	25%
9. Prices were not competitive	22%
10. Site didn't offer enough gift ideas	16%

Source: Accenture (formerly Andersen Consulting)

Support

up in the transaction process, thoroughly test your Web site. This is especially important if you are still fine-tuning the site before it's debuted. Invite some customers who will give you honest answers to test drive your site. (They'll do so with more enthusiasm if you thank them for their trouble with special discounts or conveniences.) Enlist the most representative cross-section of your customer base as possible.

As you're testing, look for these critical touchpoints, and be sure to test transactions all the way through to your customers' receipt of items.

- *Are buttons for "Help", your privacy policy, and appropriate additional information available on every page?*
- *How rapidly are customers' e-mail inquiries turned around?*
- *What questions do customers frequently ask?* (You can put the answers in your FAQ list, on appropriate Web pages, and in e-mail autorespond programs.)
- *Is the shopping cart process logical?*
- *Where are the bottlenecks in transferring customer information* from the purchase process to your customer profile databases, and vice versa?
- *How easily can customer service reps access the information* to help customers quickly via phone or e-mail?
- *Do you have a mechanism for informing customers* whether an item is in stock, back-ordered, or permanently out of stock?
- *Can your shipping system handle the additional load*, involving the input of dozens or hundreds of additional packages? (Suddenly, the feedback loop from your inventory management system, warehouse, and shipping will be condensed.)
- *Do you have enough supplies and personnel*—pickers, packers, packaging materials, gift wrap, thank-you notes, and labels?

These issues should be resolved before you go live, and you should test them regularly once your site is up and running.

Start simple. Because customer relationship management is such a convoluted affair, there is no simple, one-shot solution. You might even decide to keep your Web site very simple and encourage customers to call your customer service reps. Most sites, however, start with a basic array of customer service tools—e-mail, a phone number, rich content, and automated transaction confirmation—and then track customers' use of the site to see where it's best to add more service tools.

As you better understand how your customers use the Internet and your site in particular, you'll be able to add tools that serve them when and where they need service. Many companies are springing up to offer outsourced customer care centers that offer support through phones, e-mail, and online chat and voice contact. You can link your site to their centers and instantly offer all those functions. And as you gather more information about your customers, you'll have a richer database. That provides a solid base for e-mail campaigns, customer follow-up, and special offers. As you gain experience, you'll be able to leverage the power of the Internet—from simple tools like e-mail, to the latest integrated voice-over-Internet software—to keep your customers coming back.

Privacy and good service. Yes, customers want it all. They like it when a personalized greeting pops up when they return to a favorite site. And they love it when a site offers them free shipping as a thank-you for placing their fifth order. But, online shoppers are also wary of sharing personal information. The trick for e-commerce managers is to find the right balance. A study published in April 2000 by the Personalization Consortium, a Wakefield, Mass., trade group for electronic marketers, shows that customers do understand the tradeoff, and that, generally, they will offer some personal information to get a faster, more convenient shopping experience. In particular, 73% of consumers find it helpful when a site "remembers" basic information about them; they don't like re-entering their names and passwords. But 51% reported that they did read the fine print of sites' privacy policies before they typed in so much as one syllable of their e-mail addresses.

The more relevant the information, the more willing consumers are to divulge it. The consortium's research found that 96% of visitors would reveal their names, 95% their e-mail addresses, 81% their mailing addresses, and 76% their hobbies and interests.

At the same time, consumers are not nearly as willing to share their financial information. An unrelated survey by Cyber Dialogue, an Internet CRM company based in New York, indicates that 85% of online shoppers say that security is extremely important.

The key to treading the fine line of online privacy is to make sure that the information you're asking for is clearly relevant to the customer's convenience, says Aaron Newman, CEO of Wax Digital, a New York Web design firm. "Customers want instant gratification. They're going there [to a site] for the convenience," he says. Information to store in a "my own" section of your site might include preferred shipping addresses, sizes, important gift-giving dates, a list of items ordered in the past, and special offers that reflect buying preferences. As a retailer, you should store credit-card numbers on your site only if you can guarantee their security behind a firewall. Consider hiring an Internet security consultant to help you set up a program to monitor your site for signs of fraudulent credit-card use and security breaches.

Online fishmarket sets CRM standard. Few products have less margin for error than fresh seafood. Delivered just a few hours too late, it becomes odiferous trash accompanied by a hefty price tag. Stratis Morfogen was determined to find a way to deliver fresh seafood nationally, and along the way, developed an Internet company renowned for its customer service.

FultonStreet.com, based in New York City, informs customers of the status of their orders at every point along the way. Customer comments have inspired continual improvements of the site from the way it is organized to how much the company charges for shipping. And CEO Morfogen is relentless in seeking out new technologies to make his customers' lives even easier. First, he thought about how retail seafood consumers would want to be served through the Internet. Then, he developed customer service software and rep training materials at the same time, so they would closely coordinate. Now Morfogen carefully tracks customers' questions, problems, and suggestions to continually make changes that ensure customer satisfaction.

TIP It may seem like an obvious exercise, but be sure to study popular retail sites, including those of your competitors, to see why they feel inviting to online users, how the sites are organized, and how they offer various forms of customer service. Keep a log of good and bad features. Many of the techniques and software tools can be adapted for your own site.

In 1997, Morfogen realized that if he could solve the considerable problems of processing, order fulfillment, and shipping, he could build a tidy business buying seafood and selling it online for overnight delivery. "Two-thirds of America is landlocked and they can't get access to fish like this," he enthuses. "With an online 'front window' we can reach everyone."

Morfogen hired Vanguard InterActive, a Web development firm, to develop a customized fulfillment and order-tracking system. "Fulfillment had to be in-house—it couldn't be outsourced," Morfogen explains. "With a perishable product that people are going to eat, you can't rely on a call center to answer questions. These people (service reps) have to be well versed and trained."

Early service training. Morfogen started developing his service training program before the Web site went live, by opening up a test Internet site supported by two toll-free phone lines for orders (1-888-LOBTAIL). His first customer service reps tracked every inquiry to find out what customers wanted to know. They compiled the comments into reports for suggested changes. Their feedback resulted in "Gino the maitre d'," a software package that builds personalized files for each customer based on customer's prior questions and orders.

FultonStreet.com was unveiled in September 1998, and Gino was an instant hit. First-time customers receive a hand-crafted e-mail thanking them for their order. Then, each new customer's automated file starts to build. When an order is shipped, Gino sends an e-mail with an order-tracking number and estimated time of delivery. When the package arrives, Gino forwards a note indicating who signed for it, and when. And after the tilapia, presumably, has been grilled and consumed, Gino asks the consumer how it was. A record of all messages and responses is kept in an electronic file for each customer.

Real-time help. Though FultonStreet.com has received kudos for its customer service, Morfogen keeps refining the operation to improve it. In mid-1999, he introduced a software package that "shadows" a visitor through the site. About 10% of customers turn to this program, NetAgent, produced by eShare Technologies, for follow-up questions. Most often, they want to know if they can slip an additional item into an already completed order.

To activate NetAgent, shoppers click a button labeled "Live Help," which causes a window to pop up. The window creates a space for online chat between the customer and a FultonStreet.com rep. If the customer is looking for a particular item, the rep can make that item appear on the customer's screen by pressing a few buttons. Or, if the customer doesn't have time to chat, his or her question can be answered through e-mail.

All of these options appear on the customer service rep's screen. The rep can also call up archives of answers to frequently asked questions, scripts to lead customers through various explanations, and other resources. Each rep can help several online customers at one time.

Tracking customer questions. Meanwhile, managers have NetAgent categorize various questions so they can see where customers are getting confused on the Web site. They can compile reports on interactive traffic patterns, customers' preferred methods of communicating, and how efficient the reps are.

Armed with details from the NetAgent reports, Morfogen gave FultonStreet.com an overhaul. One revelation: He thought that the $9.99 flat-rate shipping was great, but customers disagreed. After Morfogen expanded the store's offerings to include New York deli staples, some customers simply wanted to order a $6 jar of marmalade. Obviously, the $9.99 shipping fee discouraged that. So, Morfogen tweaked the fee rates, adding a $4.95 rate for orders under $20—and making shipping free for Manhatten residents. "Now people are ordering lots of little items. It's huge!" he says.

FultonStreet.com started out in a 500-square-foot office. Now, its perishables processing plant sprawls over 144,000 square feet. Morfogen employs 35 people year-round and 30 more at the peak seasons. And, Morfogen has converted expertise in keeping fresh things fresh over long distances into a profitable business-to-business service. He now handles the fulfillment functions for the gourmet food offerings of 1-800-FLOWERS and several other online stores that wanted to expand into food items.

Instead of expecting customers to comform to his Web site's capabilities, Morfogen paid close attention to their questions and shaped his site to reflect their needs. As a result, he is now recognized as an expert in Web customer service. Just as important, the financial performance of

FultonStreet.com is so promising that investors have poured more money into it. They are counting on Morfogen's ability to spread his gospel of customer service to other companies, and make money doing it. ∎

COMPANIES AND SITES IN THIS CHAPTER

Advantage Credit International
www.advantagecredit.com

Accenture **www.accenture.com**

Cyber Dialogue **www.cyberdialogue.com**

eShare Technologies **www.eshare.com**

FultonStreet.com **www.fultonstreet.com**

Personalization Consortium
www.personalization.org

Resource Marketing
www.resource.com

Vanguard InterActive
www.vanguardinteractive.com

Wax Digital **www.waxdigital.com**

Support

Chapter 2

E-mail: Why It's the Universal Tool

Internet experts don't call e-mail "the killer app" for nothing. It's extremely easy to use by both staff and customers; it can be saved for future reference through a variety of means; and it doesn't require a sophisticated technical set-up.

According to Forrester Research, a technology research and analysis firm in Cambridge, Mass., e-mail is the single most effective electronic tool for strengthening customer relationships. Besides offering instant value, it can time offers of your products or services for maximum results and increase repeat sales. Forrester estimates that by 2004, more than two-thirds of the e-mails sent to customers will be geared towards keeping them, not acquiring them.

This chapter explores basic ways that you can leverage the convenience and power of e-mail to communicate with your customers. It focuses on how to maximize features embedded in standard Internet browsers, how to organize and track e-mail communiques, how to train staff in e-mail usage, and, most importantly, how to use e-mail in a way that genuinely serves your customers.

Keep in mind that e-mail is a unique tool that also can be used to address other customer relationship management (CRM) issues—for example, responding to a request for warranty information or explaining when a shipment will arrive. Some e-mail responses may be as simple as directing a customer to a particular page on your Web site, while other e-mails will lead to a phone conversation between customer and service rep to answer complicated questions. Customers don't care so much about the means you use to respond to them, as long as you reply—promptly.

Immediate access, anywhere. One reason why e-mail is so popular is that

E-mail

nearly anyone can use it, anywhere. That's not just true for business travelers who are used to logging on at hotels and airport business centers while they're on the road. Even people who don't have computers can get free e-mail through services like Juno and Yahoo and check in through computers at public libraries, community centers, and cybercafes. When you have someone's e-mail address, you have a way of communicating with them directly, without playing phone tag.

Universal access to e-mail cuts both ways. When customers see that you are available via e-mail—even if you don't have a Web site—they will assume that you're checking your e-mail account frequently. No matter where they are, or where you are, they'll expect you to respond to their e-mails right away. Failure to do so earns very few second chances.

Key e-mail functions. Chances are you're using an Internet browser such as Netscape, Microsoft's Outlook, or AOL for e-mail. E-mail functions are also being added to sales support software programs such as GoldMine and Symantec's ACT!. Another popular and easy-to-use e-mail program is Qualcomm's Eudora. All of these software programs offer basic tools that let you screen, file, and organize e-mail. If your company is very small, or if you have relatively few clients, you may not need

TIP Jupiter Research, a New York Internet analysis firm, found that 40% of the companies it surveyed either didn't respond to customers' e-mails at all, or took up to five days to respond. Companies that deliver on their promise to respond to e-mail queries within 4, 6, or 24 hours (whatever they believe is appropriate for their business) can take advantage of the carelessness of those that don't respond to capture customers' attention, loyalty—and orders.

E-mail

much more than the simple database functions embedded in these e-mail programs to manage your customer contacts. Among the most common functions are these:

• *Multiple personalities*. Set up different e-mail accounts for specific brands, locations, or projects (e.g., bbq@hotsauce.com or sizingquestions@ swimsuits.com). This enables you to automatically forward e-mails to a specific person in your company assigned to answer them. The specific e-mail addresses can be posted at the appropriate places on your Web site.

• *Filters*. Create sub-categories in your mailbox so that mail is auto-matically deposited in, say, each client's or project's slot. Anything that comes in from a particular e-mail address will automatically be deposited there. You can also tell clients to flag urgent messages with a certain tagline—such as "urgent"—and set up a box to receive only those. This enables you to prioritize your e-mail flow.

• *In-boxes*. Even if you don't use filters, you can still build archives of e-mails on particular topics, or projects, or from certain people, by creating internal in-boxes. One of your employees simply drags the e-mail from your general in-box to a more specific one. This is useful for keeping track of "conversations" you may be having with clients, and ensures that you can refer back to requests—and your responses. If you want to broadcast an e-mail to everyone who has corresponded with you on a particular topic, you can use the topic-specific in-box as a defacto e-mail list.

• *Templates*. Called "stationery" in Eudora, this function lets you create boilerplate messages and simply plug in the recipient's e-mail address. This is excellent for answering standard questions, such as driving directions to your office. However, if you find that certain questions are asked very often, you may want to post the answer on the frequently-asked-questions (FAQ) list on your Web site.

E-mail

TIP Ask your managers to answer a minimum number of random customer e-mails weekly. This is the equivalent of a free-associating focus group. Managers will get a thumbnail picture of what's on your customers' minds and how well your site and customer service efforts are addressing customers' concerns and demands.

• *Auto-respond*. This function bounces back a canned answer to a general e-mail. Most basic browser e-mail functions will only let you send out an "I'm not here" message that explains why you're not going to respond to the e-mail. More sophisticated programs let you craft different autoresponds tailored to the customer's request or order history.

• *Embedded links*. Use the "link" function to connect customers with a Web page within your site or at another site. The e-mail will be sent in HTML format and the customer can click on the highlighted link to be transported immediately to that page. This is an easy way to direct customers to a particular page on your site that they may not have been able to find.

No matter how you organize the e-mail that flows into your business, think about what type of response customers are likely to expect. If they're making a routine inquiry, such as asking if you carry a certain brand of sneakers, short and snappy is fine. But if you're staking your reputation on highly customized, expensive products or services, be sure to give a "you're special" tone to your responses.

"We answer every e-mail that comes through the door," says Susan Rossie, vice president of Susan Fredman & Associates, a residential and commercial interior design firm in Northbrook, Ill. Rossie says that because her clients expect completely personalized services, the staff divides up the responsibility of responding, asking specifically what type of follow-up potential clients prefer (e.g., an appointment or printed introductory material in the mail). Rossie says that busy two-income clients often initiate their very first contact with the company through its Web site, especially late at night and on weekends, when the staff isn't around to handle phone calls. Every e-mail contact is considered a chance to win or serve a customer.

Provide insider contacts. Another way to win customers is to be quick on your feet. Because such a high proportion of companies are lax in managing their e-mail, you can use prompt, targeted e-mail responses as a key tool to differentiate you from your competitors. One way to do that is to post a directory of employees' names, titles, and e-mail addresses on your Web site,

POST YOUR E-MAIL ADDRESS EVERYWHERE

You never know when a customer will feel the urge to reach out to you with a question, complaint, repeat order, or compliment. Make it easy for your customers to send you an e-mail by promoting your online presence in as many offline venues as possible. Be sure even your basic marketing materials, such as those listed below, carry your Web and/or e-mail addresses as well as your USPS address and phone number.

- stationery
- business cards
- invoices and statements
- packing slips
- graph or design paper
- follow-up surveys
- evaluation forms

- rubber address stamps
- boxes, bags, packaging
- direct mail flyers
- premiums and giveaways
- Yellow Pages ad
- window signs
- vehicles

(some companies even include home phone numbers). As a result, customers' e-mails are more likely to land on the right desk the first time, rather than being forwarded around the company. An employee directory also communicates your genuine desire to build relationships with your customers.

Tracking e-mail. It's easy for e-mails to be lost in an electronic shuffle. An inquiry received in a general mailbox for example, may be forwarded to someone in technical support and then passed on to the marketing department. You can get raw data on the number of e-mails that flow into your Web site from your Internet service provider (ISP) or into your server from its logs allowing you to track daily volume. Keeping track of a specific e-mail as it travels around your company, however, is more complicated.

If you receive only occasional queries, have an employee respond and send a copy of the response to you. You can drop it into your own folder of communications with that customer for future reference. This is not practical, though, for large volumes of e-mail. If you don't want to invest in a full-fledged database program or subscribe to a database service, have an administrative assistant maintain a master e-mail list. However, you'll find that maintaining more than over 150 or so customer contacts and/or more than three dozen e-mail folders becomes unwieldy, making it necessary to upgrade to a full-fledged contact management program.

The most powerful versions of GoldMine and ACT! enable users to create centralized libraries of contacts, archived e-mails and responses, and documents for automatic or quick response. By using programs such as these, employees can copy well-crafted letters sent by others; see what was sent, to whom, and when, and easily update critical addresses when they notice that someone's e-mail address has changed. Of course, in order for everyone in the company to have access to the e-mail center, your computers must be networked.

Clean house regularly. Brace yourself for the constant maintenance required to keep your e-mail databases clear of invalid addresses. If you maintain your list in-house, a staffer will have to spend part of every day scanning through e-mails to remove the addresses of people who want to be taken off your list.

Assign an administrative assistant to collaborate closely with the employees who use the database most often to be sure that you're streamlining customer contact information at every point. Customer identification numbers should be consistent across all orders, databases, and customer touchpoints, including e-mail. That way, a customer who calls on the phone to take advantage of a frequent-buyer offer received through e-mail can be recognized and accommodated. This is best accomplished by having a single customer database that's used by all departments. The last thing you want is to have your sales department, for example, create its own database—one that can't be merged with the inventory system in the warehouse used for picking orders generated through your Web site.

Cultivate good netiquette. Your company's reputation can be enhanced or eroded with every e-mail. Sales, marketing, and customer service staffers, in particular, represent your company every time they send out an e-mail to

E-mail

a customer, supplier, or partner.

No matter how well your employee knows a recipient, you should make it clear that forwarding tacky jokes, chain letters, the URLs or links for controversial sites, and similar electronic flotsam is not acceptable. Even so, the most sincerely well-meaning e-mails can appear sloppy and unprofessional if the sender doesn't bother to use proper capitalization or run the message through a spell-check. Casual grammar, poor sentence structure, and mistaken punctuation may seem friendly and conversational, but e.e.cummings-style notes carelessly banged out by a customer service rep will appear sloppy to recipients. So will confusing online acronyms favored by people who frequent listservers and bulletin boards (for example, "LOL" for "laughing out loud").

Create a style guide. It's important to help your managers develop a style sheet that reps can use for live chat, instant messaging, and e-mail responses. That way, they'll give customers consistant, straightforward, helpful responses and won't be tempted to lapse into Web culture shorthand.

And what about "emoticons," those cutesy arrangements of punctuation marks to indicate smiley faces and other emotions? They are commonly used and understood, but they're not professional looking. It's up to you whether to ban or welcome the smiley face.

A thoughtfully crafted e-mail can go a long way to build or repair customer opinions of your company. It can even say, "I'm sorry." In February 2000, Egreetings Network, an online greeting card service, embarrassed itself by fluffing the transmission of electronic valentines that customers had ordered days and weeks in advance. Chief operating office Gordon Tucker sent out an apology on February 17, offering to take the blame for bruised hearts. "We're truly sorry for the inconvenience we caused you, and we encourage you to forward this letter to your friend, sweetheart, or family member so that they know that it was our fault they didn't get their greeting on time," he wrote. "We're doing everything possible to keep a delay like this from ever happening again. We value you as a customer and hope that you will give us another chance."

It proved to be one way to make lemonade from lemons. ■

COMPANIES AND SITES IN THIS CHAPTER

AOL **www.aol.com**

Egreetings Network **www.egreetings.com**

Eudora/Qualcomm **www.eudora.com**

Forrester Research **www.forrester.com**

Susan Fredman & Associates
www.susanfredman.com

GoldMine **www.goldmine.com**

Jupiter Research **www.jup.com**

Microsoft **www.microsoft.com**

Netscape **www.netscape.com**

Symantec **www.symantec.com**

Yahoo **www.yahoo.com**

E-mail

Chapter 3

Database-driven E-mail

Once you have gained a customer, it's up to you to build a relationship. The more he or she purchases from you, the more information you can collect—and the more variables you have to improve your service and earn the customer's loyalty. This chapter explores the pros and cons of switching from a relatively simple database—of the sort that is included in desktop and simple network office management packages and contact management software—to more sophisticated options. And as you build your database capabilities, you should increase your customer service content correspondingly. Without heads-up service, you'll simply have a more powerful engine (the database)—but no roadmap for using it strategically.

Stepping up your database. Databases enable you to compile vast amounts of information about customers so that you can come closer to giving each individual precisely targeted information. For instance, a car dealership might send all its customers a small booklet that includes an annual maintenance schedule for all the car models it sells, at a cost of $1 per customer. But by leveraging a database, the dealership could send each customer an oversized postcard that lists the maintenance schedule for the model that car owner bought, at the lower cost of only 40¢ each. The costs drop even lower—perhaps as little as 10¢ each—if the dealer has the e-mail addresses of its customers and can send each one a digital postcard in a rich e-mail format that looks just like a printed postcard.

You should consider upgrading your database if:

• *You have more than 500 customers.*

• *You don't want to limit the number of "fields,"* or individual bits of information, about each customer.

• *Your employees want to create customized e-mails for their accounts.*

• *You are upgrading your network* and hiring a consultant anyway.

• *You are aggressively ramping up sales,* which will touch off in-house demand for information about customers for follow-up marketing and customer service.

• *You are adding or expanding transactional capabilities* on your Web site and soon must make customer account information available to service reps who may be working on the phone, in e-mail, real-time chat, and real-time messaging.

• *You want to add search functions to your company intranet* so that employees can quickly find customer information.

Database manager. Unless you already have a database manager who can install an upgraded system, troubleshoot it, and train employees, you probably need to hire a consultant. As you consider the choice of your database manager, keep in mind your long-term objectives for the database: One goal may be to drive down the cost of customer communication by moving as much as possible to e-mail. You should also consider the scope of your growth plans, the new markets you are pursuing, and the amount of money you can afford to spend on the database. You will need to continually upgrade the database, enter new information, maintain it, and train employees on squeezing the most from it.

One database management program that can automatically integrate e-mail received through your Web site with Microsoft's Access database is PostCast. Another option is to step up to a more complex version of a database system you're already using; for example, Microsoft's SQL technology has similar user interfaces for its desktop and server versions. Companies upgrading to the latest SQL version don't have to start training employees from scratch and will have fewer hassles transferring data from the old system to the new one. Similar options are available with Sybase's SQL database packages and IBM's Netfinity 3000.

Database services. According to some technology research experts, companies that use e-mail service bureaus for marketing can get up to four times the purchase rate from customers who receive e-mails, compared to companies that keep their e-mail marketing operations in-house. Managing a database is complicated and time-consuming. If you see multiple synergies between your offline and online marketing and customer relationship management, it may be well worth it to integrate all your customer contact databases into one that offers employees multiple ways of using the data.

When you sign up with an e-mail service provider, the provider will arrange for your current e-mail database to be converted to its database. Typically, the CGI script that underlies many Web sites and related e-mail can be easily formatted to make the transition to link online with your Web site so that e-mails generated there go to the e-mail service provider. Typically, these will be requests to be on your promotional, notification, and news e-mail lists. You'll need to specify which e-mails, though, should be sent directly to your customer service reps, such as questions about product returns that can't be answered by the database management staff. While the data belongs to you, it resides both with the outsourcer and on your company's computers, thanks to regular downloads of updated files. Part of your contract with the outsourcer should specify back-ups at regular intervals and secure transmission of updates to your computer's database. (If your office computers have a slow Internet connection, this may be problematic; in that case, request database updates on CD-ROM or disk.)

Outsourcer's reports. The updates can be poured into a file that has the same format and technical protocols as the one used by the outsourcer, who can also train your staff on how to extract reports from it. But, much of the value of using an e-mail outsourcer is having its staff produce reports. Besides performing routine functions such as removing duplicate addresses, an e-mail outsourcer can also help you understand exactly what type of e-mails your site is sending out. For instance, if you post an offer on your Web site for instructions on new ways to use a product you sell, and get 5,000 requests for the subsequent e-mail, the service provider can tell you when those requests come in, what ZIP codes they represent, and what other products those particular customers have purchased from you. Variables like these can help you understand how your customers are using your products and what related products and services you might be able to sell them.

Other reports include the number of "subscribes" and "unsubscribe" requests from customers; how readers link back to your site through links in e-mails you've sent them; if readers are forwarding your e-mails to friends (and who those friends are); and specific domain names that receive your e-mails (so that you can screen out e-mails from competitors). You can also create reports that profile contact with each customer, including questions, purchases, returns, and responses to e-mails.

Outsourcing options. You have two options for arranging outsourced e-mail database management and broadcasting: Keep the e-mail function separate from your Web hosting service, or have your Internet service provider (ISP) handle it. If you keep the function separate and use a service such as e2 Communications, Maximum Broadcasting, or Exstream Data, you'll have the service provider take the content of e-mails you want to send, format it, and send it to everyone you specify on your e-mail list. A typical cost for that kind of service is about 10¢ to 15¢ for each e-mail.

However, the outsourcer will also have to coordinate with your Web developer and the ISP that hosts your Web site to ensure that data posted at the site—for example, customers' registration information—is automatically captured by the ISP and forwarded to your files maintained by the e-mail outsourcer. Once this is set up, the ISP's e-mail files will serve as a backup, and the ones maintained by the outsourcer can be mined for information.

If your ISP offers e-mail and database management functions, you can capitalize on your existing relationship by adding that to the services you're already paying for. You'll have one large database that can be used for all kinds of customer reporting and e-mail broadcasting—but beware that the ISP may not have staffers who specialize just in e-mail broadcasting to help you fine-tune your campaigns.

Both e-mail outsourcers and ISP's have much faster Internet connections than most small businesses have. Unless you have a T-1 line and are

SHOULD YOU GO OUTSIDE FOR DATABASE SERVICES?

Advantages	Disadvantages
Monthly subscription helps you manage cash flow.	Your data is held in another company's computers, which could invoke security issues.
You gain immediate access to latest upgrades in database technology.	Access to database experts might become limited or expensive.
Minimal training is required for your employees.	You must constantly explain your industry trends, customer service, and e-mail goals to the outsourcer.
Internet-based services enable your sales reps to access client data while working remotely.	Possible limitations on accessing your database files: Internet-based service may prohibit you from saving your files on your computer, or if the outsourcer's network is down, you lose access to your files.

willing to assign a staffer to oversee the transmission of broadcast e-mails late at night (when telecommunications lines are less crowded), it may be worthwhile to outsource the transmission just to avoid tying up your company's computers and data lines for hours at a time.

The chart on the opposite page compares the advantages and disadvantages of hiring an outside database management service.

Collecting customer data. In completing a transaction, a customer generates valuable information—from name to e-mail address. You may already have much of that information in another database collected for a direct mail campaign or customer follow-up. Chances are, though, that you don't have e-mail addresses as part of the information on each customer in your old database. You'll have to decide if you want to create an entirely new database that is solely developed from customers who contact you through e-mail or your Web site (and who fill out a new form), or if you will capture the e-mail addresses from current customers who visit your site and then add those to your pre-existing database. That can be done simply by creating an e-mail field in the customer file format in your current database and assigning a support staffer to screen incoming e-mails for those from current customers, then copy the e-mail addresses from the address line and dropping it into the field in your existing database.

TIP If you choose to add e-mail addresses to your existing database, check the compatibility of your database program with the technical capacities of the e-mail management program you're considering buying, before you spend the money. Some database programs are so dated that they can't easily be linked to a powerful e-mail management program.

One significant advantage of enriching your current database is that you will have all customer contact information in one place. As customers start to view sales made over the Internet less as a novelty and more as a convenience, they will expect you to have complete records of all their transactions at every touchpoint: e-mail, real-time chat, phone, fax, and regular mail. If your goal is to provide seamless, consistent customer service, carefully consider how you will continually improve and integrate access to customer data from all these touchpoints.

Database content. Your marketing and customer service teams should collaborate closely to decide what information to include in the database for e-mail campaigns. Besides basic contact and address information, options may include customer-specific data such as:

- *Account activity, including prior purchases.*
- *Preferences on receiving future offers, maintenance services, and reminder.*
- *Response via mail, e-mail, or a form on your Web site.*
- *Personal reminder service, such as for birthdays.*
- *Customer requests to be notified of the availability of additional products* or ones similar or complementary to the items that the customer has already purchased.
- *Questions the customer asked your service rep* as he or she shopped or discussed a transaction.

Content drives contacts. Customers appreciate e-mails that clearly indicate that you think about them personally (instead of just slapping their name on a generic promotional notice). Developing e-mail content that's useful but not intrusive is a constant balancing act.

"Ask not what you want to say to your customer, but what they want to hear from you," advises Hans Peter Brøndmo, founder of Post Communications, a San Francisco firm that specializes in customized e-mail marketing programs. "Why do your customers want your e-mails? If you can't come up with a good answer, then why will someone want to hear about a news item?"

Review prior successful direct mail campaigns for ideas of what customers may find relevant and useful in an e-mail update. If customers respond in droves to coupons offering free breadsticks with any order of a large pizza, they'll probably go for similar deals announced via e-mail. You should also invite their suggestions for discounts, giveaways, tips, and information through a page on your Web site that includes a pop-up e-mail box or small survey to fill out. Another approach is to offer several types of follow-up that customers can choose, or opt into, such as how-tos for the products they've purchased, notices about related items as they become available, or information about sales.

TIP The average U.S. Internet user received 40 commercial e-mails in 1999 but will be deluged with 1,600 by 2005, according to Jupiter Research, an e-commerce analysis firm in New York. Value-conscious American consumers will become increasingly choosy about which e-mails they will read and which ones they consider nuisances. Response rates will drop dramatically for e-mails that are considered irrelevant, too pushy, or too intrusive.

Added value. That's the driving force that has resulted in the Women's Consumer Network (WCN), an online buying service that meticulously researches consumer goods and services and then negotiates deals for its members for the best of the crop. The appeal of the WCN is that consumers not only can use its proprietary analysis of products and services as a buying guide, but credibility is enhanced by the added value of seeing the "homework" that its staff conducts, especially since WCN plans to sell advertising on the site. Instead of simply recommending a product or service, WCN spells out the pros and cons of buying a cell phone subscription, a mortgage online, and popular home electronics, for example.

WCN president and founder Melissa Moss knew she'd have to explain her concept thoroughly to persuade consumers to pay a $21.95 annual membership fee. Lucid e-mails embedded with links that invite action, sent consistently, are the cornerstone of her ongoing efforts to establish the service as a consumer staple.

"I expect that members will e-mail us questions," says Moss, whose customer service reps are continually adding to their searchable library of canned responses that they can cut and paste into e-mails. For instance, a site visitor who asks about how to choose a financial planner will be sent a list of criteria that the WCN staff used as it analyzed financial planners, including the availability of "fully-trained counselors by phone during business hours and custom reports based on your needs, for an extra fee."

"There's the expectation that the e-mail will be answered immediately," says Moss. "But it works both ways. A quick response stokes interest in pursuing the purchase right away. A delayed reply often means a lost sale."

E-mail tree. Moss is also leveraging WCN's e-mail campaigns to encourage members to sign up their friends. Simple tools, such as encouraging members to forward introductory e-mails, are proving effective. By the end of 1999, more than 45,000 women had signed up for the service and were starting to report on the results of their newly acquired knowledge. One consumer saved $2,000 on the purchase of a new car—an amount that clearly justifies her continued membership for years to come.

If you're not sure if your staff can generate e-mails with an element that triggers direct-response action, consider hiring an outside copy writer or consultant who can help you fashion some standard formats for invoking response from e-mail recipients.

Rich e-mail. Most Internet users have been accustomed to receiving e-mail in plain text format. But as Web sites have become more sophisticated, so are e-mails. Options such as graphics, embedded video and audio that are enacted with a click, and the ability to respond to the e-mail without going back to the original Web site being offered by cutting-edge direct mail and advertising firms that specialize in Internet marketing.

The free daily e-mail update sent by ClickZ, a consulting firm that organizes conferences on Internet marketing and advertising, is a well-designed mosaic of color banners, clearly defined (and brief) pitches from sponsors, articles by columnists, and links to the editors' picks of the best articles appearing that day elsewhere on the Web. Rich e-mails, which are essentially a 'live' Web page delivered to the recipient's e-mail box, are created and formatted using standard HTML and Web design tools (compared with simple text format, which is far less appealing).

TIP Rich e-mail is most useful to customers with fast Internet connections. If you suspect that many of your customers don't have fast connections, offer them the option of receiving a text format e-mail or a rich e-mail when they initially sign up. Trip.com, a travel Web site, has a simple, easy-to-understand format for helping visitors choose which format they prefer—rich e-mail or text—for its newsletters. Most people are more impressed by an e-mail message that specifically addresses their own needs than with fancy technology, unless that technology makes their communication with your company significantly easier.

Create an e-mail newsletter. Producing the first edition of a newsletter can be fun. It gives you a format for information you want to convey to customers, feeds the perception that you are anticipating their needs, and differentiates you from competitors that use plain boilerplate e-mail. You can format the newsletter in a variety of ways; from a simple, plain-text version that's created in a word processing document and pasted into a standard e-mail, to a graphically attractive newsletter that appears in full form on your Web site (to which customers are invited via an e-mail that links back to it).

Customer-care consultant Patricia Seybold has a hybrid approach for her eNewsletter, which is e-mailed in plain text. Links back to Seybold's Web site appear early in the newsletter so that recipient's who want to read it in a fancier format can click back to it. Next come brief headliners of new white papers, articles, and reports, followed by three- or four-paragraph descriptions of the new items listed. The newsletter always ends with a short paragraph about the company and Seybold, the name and phone number of the company's customer service supervisor, and a link where recipients can unsubscribe.

A graphically fancier, but equally well-organized, newsletter is the *Internet Advertising Report* generated daily by internet.com, a company that publishes research, statistics, and newsletters about e-commerce. The newsletter includes a link to its own archives—a value-added convenience for readers who may want to learn more about a company mentioned in that day's news. Each of the five to seven feature articles has a headline that also serves as a highlighted link; readers can click on the headline to open up a box with the entire story, then click back to continue scrolling through other headlines in the newsletter. A complete list of other topics that internet.com covers appears in a box that runs along the left margin, the better to encourage reader exploration of the company's additional services.

Keeping a newsletter going is a lot of work. By the third edition, your employees may be scratching for relevant news. There's a fine line between a marketing e-mail newsletter and one that specifically supports the customer. But once a customer has purchased from you, then you can provide additional information about the product or service. You can provide ideas on additional ways to use things (e.g., from used computers to treadmills); offer specials on refills (e.g., cosmetics), and send reminders about upcoming events, such as routine car maintenance or seasonal gardening tips.

Permission counts. When customers find your messages genuinely useful, they will eagerly anticipate, open, and act on your e-mails. But don't take advantage of customer goodwill. Even if you already have a database of e-mail addresses, you will want to elicit the permission of those customers before automatically putting them on your e-mail list. It's fine to send out an introductory e-mail, but go no further unless you have a recipient's buy-in.

Marketing consultant Seth Godin champions the concept of eliciting a "yes!" from consumers before signing them up for any sort of follow-up. "Opt-in" is the term for requesting customers to specifically ask to be put on your list. "Opt-out" is the term for assuming that customers are granting permission when they give you their e-mail address for any purpose at all, even if it is just sending an inquiry or signing a guest book. They are assumed to be signing up for future mailings unless they specifically "opt out."

Opt out/opt in. Aggressive e-mail marketers adopt the opt-out tactic—that customers who don't respond at all are giving their tacit approval for future e-mails. The trouble with that is that many customers won't scroll far enough down the e-mail to see your advise on how to take action to get off your regular mailing list. If they can't figure out how to get off the list, they'll simply get in the habit of automatically deleting any e-mail you send.

A more painstaking, but ultimately more productive, tactic is opt-in.

HOW TO MAKE AN E-MAIL NEWSLETTER CLICK

Here are eight tips for producing a newsletter that will win your company praise as a customer service organization:

1. Make the content broad, flexible, and relevant. Each item you include must have genuine, stand-alone value to the customer. Does the message make any sense if you eliminate your company as its source? For instance, it may be exciting to you that your offices have been refurbished, but few customers are likely to share your enthusiasm. On the other hand, a new system for making client reservations and managing appointments to minimize the time clients spend in those offices is exactly what customers want. Don't just brag about the capacity of the appointment scheduler—tell customers how they, specifically, can make it work for them (e.g., now they can leave voice-mail messages and be assured that they'll get a return call confirming one of their requested appointment times).

2. Make it one person's responsibility. Assign the development, writing, and production of your customer newsletter to someone who has a knack for seeing the customer's viewpoint and works well with others in your company. Encourage your newsletter editor to seek out information, angles, and customer testimonials that will be of use to other customers.

3. Keep it short. Most newsletters include only one or two "feature" articles (usually no longer than 500 words each) and a handful of very short newsy items. If part of your goal is to draw people back to your company Web site, include only a two- or three-sentence summary of each feature, accompanied by a hotlink directly to the newsletter's "home" on your company's site.

4. Keep the graphics simple. Because customers' e-mail systems vary so widely, resist the temptation to create a graphics-heavy, fancy newsletter. The simplest and most universally acceptable method is all text. Use dashes, asterisks, and punctuation marks to delineate stories and announcements. Keep the width of the text to a maximum of 60 characters so that readers can quickly scan through the contents without fully opening their e-mail browsers.

5. Include instructions. Tell customers how to get off the mailing list, or give them a link at least to those instructions on your Web site.

6. Provide response mechanisms. It's relatively easy to weave direct-response mechanisms into the newsletter. Mentions of a new product can be accompanied by direct hotlinks to the sales managers for that product. If you're clearing out overstocks, link directly to the bargains page. Your Webmaster or Internet service provider will be able to help you structure reports that indicate what traffic was generated by the e-mail links.

7. Dig in for the long haul. There will be times when it seems you have way too much good material for the newsletter format you've chosen, and other times when you can barely fill out that format. Encourage your newsletter editor to steadily collect interesting information so customers will always receive worthwhile content.

8. Archive old issues online. Past issues of the newsletter may be of interest to customers if they are trying to unearth a description of one of your products that you sent out months ago. At the very least, archive issues by date. It's more expensive, but exponentially more helpful, to add a search function for the archives. If that's not feasible, at least have the editor create an index, categorizing articles by two or three keywords so that customers can find them relatively quickly.

Briefly outline the benefits that customers will get by actively choosing to be on your e-mail list (advance notice of sales, first to hear breaking news, etc.) and then provide a response mechanism for them to put themselves on your list. Usually that mechanism is to simply hit "reply" and put in the message line "subscribe." Or, you might take the opportunity to capture more information and ask customers to click on a link to your site, where you've installed a short questionnaire for them to fill out. WomenCONNECT.com, a provider of resources for women in business, invites visitors to fill out a brief questionnaire when they click on the link to sign up for its newsletter. Just make sure you don't make the response mechanism too burdensome, or you'll lose a high proportion of your customers along the way.

Customers are much more likely to say "yes!" if they know exactly what they are signing up for. Specifically outline what e-mails they will get from you if they sign up for notices or a newsletter. Amy Gahran's online magazine *Contentious*, at www.contentious.com, positions the opt-in process at the top center of the home page. When visitors click on that, the sign-up page clearly delineates the nature of the e-mail updates she sends out, the privacy policy, and a link to a pop-up box to contact Gahran.

TIP The more complex or expensive the items you are selling, the more valuable a completely personal, albeit slower, response will be to interested customers. It's worth it to offer one-on-one help via phone or e-mail for items that aren't likely to be impulse purchases. Conversely, inexpensive or commodity items are more likely to be purchased on the spur of the moment, so a real-time, immediate response approach to customers' queries is more appropriate.

Godin points out that a "yes" can quickly degenerate into a

determined "no!" if you, the marketer, take advantage of the granted permission. Clutter up your customers' mailboxes with e-mails that only brag about your company and that add little or no value to the customer, and you've violated your permission agreement, argues Godin.

Prompt e-mail response. E-mail has one drawback as a response mechanism at the transaction point. Even if your e-mail turnaround is as prompt as 10 minutes, that is still a 10-minute delay. And the customer will have to leave your site temporarily to pull up his or her e-mail menu and see whether your response has arrived. Even short amounts of time are long enough for a customer to grow impatient and move on to another site, or have second thoughts about the transaction altogether.

However, e-mail does offer the advantage of a completely customized response. You can partially overcome the drawbacks by clearly stating how long it will take you to respond to the customer. Explanatory text placed adjacent to the button that contains the pop-up e-mail form is the best location for this type of message because customers are more receptive to the information at this point in the purchase process.

Avoid "opt-out." In early 2000, *Consumer Reports* analyzed privacy statements at more than 50 retail Web sites. Its experts found that most sites' explanations of their privacy statements were so complicated that consumers would probably misunderstand them. The magazine's recommendation to online marketers: Don't offer opt-out as a choice at the beginning. Offer only the chance to opt-in to your database. Having opted in, a consumer should always be able to unsubscribe to any list, whether they opted in on purpose or were opted in without their explicit consent. When you offer opt-in, people make a conscious decision to subscribe to your e-mailings. However, it is essential to clearly outline in every broadcast e-mail how they can delete their name from your list.

As your customer files become more detailed, you'll have better data for targeting follow-up e-mails for cross-selling, repeat sales, and product-related services. You'll also be able to detect patterns that help you anticipate customers' needs—and address them through your Web site. ■

COMPANIES AND SITES IN THIS CHAPTER

ClickZ **www.clickz.com**

Contentious **www.contentious.com**

e2 Communications **www.e2software.com**

Exstream Data **www.exdata.com**

Seth Godin, author of *Permission Marketing* **www.permission.com**

IBM **www.ibm.com**

Internet.ccm **www.internet.com**

Maximum Broadcasting **www.maximumbroadcasting.com**

Microsoft **www.microsoft.com**

PostCast **www.postcast.com**

Post Communications **www.netcentives.com**

Patricia Seybold Group **www.psgroup.com**

Sybase **www.sybase.com**

· Chapter 4 ·

Enriched Site Content

Your Web-site content can be as simple as a well-developed, frequently-asked-question (FAQ) list in text format, or as detailed as catalog copy and downloadable forms and instructions. The acid-test: Do customers return to the site to seek content and pose questions, learning about your products and services in the process?

Kansas City executive coach Jennifer White uses her Web site partly to sell books and tapes of her speeches, but mainly for customer service—to enable clients to contact her and other coaches in her group. One popular feature is the "Ask the Coach" Q & A column. White answers some questions (for instance, "How do I stop feeling compelled to read everything that lands on my desk?"), but also lets the coaches that she has trained get exposure by answering questions and tackling clients' and readers' dilemmas.

White estimates that she saves about $3,000 in mailing costs annually by encouraging people to sign up for her seminars through the site. By collecting an e-mail address from everyone who takes the online quiz "to see if our philosophy can help you create more success in your life," as well as from those who sign up for her e-mail newsletter, White has built a database of more than 20,000 people. She had custom links built between Microsoft's Access database system and Intuit's QuickBooks accounting software to ensure that she captures the e-mail address of everyone who has ever bought a book or attended one of her workshops, so they can be offered the option of being added to her e-mail list.

Rich "passive" content. Enriched "passive" content is the useful information posted on your site to which customers refer when they are looking for answers. Think of it as standing, billboard fare, unlike interactive content. If you already know what type of information your customers like to get, and in what format, post it and invite customers to help themselves at any time of day or night. Your employees should also be able to direct customers to the appropriate "passive" sections of the site, instead of mailing or faxing them the materials.

Existing offline customer support information you may already have on hand might include:

- Instructions for using your products (projects, recipes, and other how-to's that explain additional uses for your products)
- Technical specifications about your products
- Schedules for maintenance and upgrades
- Schedules for service delivery
- Product catalogs
- Company background information
- Order/backorder status and estimated arrival time
- How to contact your customer service reps
- Directions to your office or store and business hours

Much of this information can be reorganized and placed on your Web site—a task that can be accomplished relatively quickly if you already have digital files of text, graphics, and other elements. Standard HTML can be used to make your existing information Web-ready simply and quickly. Beware, however, that the organization and layout of most printed pieces are not Web-friendly. If you simply download a brochure, for example, online visitors may have difficulty navigating through it—especially if it includes four-color pictures. Break it into simpler graphical and textual elements and place them separately on your site where people will look for them.

The "About Our Company" category is nearly universal at all business sites, so most people visiting your site will expect to see this internal link. It's the place to put all the basic introductory information about your company—

such as its history, what you do, and short bios of key managers—broken down into short segments, each with its own navigation button. Because it's important to have a consistent graphic style on your Web site and printed materials, have a designer simplify the graphics from existing materials so that they'll fit the Web format and, more importantly, download quickly.

Strategically placed "Help" options. When you're selling products that evoke many ques-

TIP Besides reorganizing the content of printed products, consider providing crosslinks between categories. For instance, a viewer who is reading a project profile can click on an embedded link in the text that leads to the bio of an executive mentioned in the profile. Crosslinks will give you maximum mileage from materials you already have and provide site visitors with the same basics that you'd hand them in person.

tions, it's important to provide information about those products right alongside the "Buy" button. In-depth product descriptions, e-mail contacts, and your toll-free phone number can supplement the ubiquitous presence of your site-wide "Help" button. This is an inexpensive way to aid customers and maximize the impact of your content.

Vitamins.com covers an extensive list of subjects under its "Help" button that appears at the top of every page—among them, how to use the shopping cart, tips on using browsers, how to order from the site through fax and mail, and payment options. Every product description is also accompanied by buttons that introduce the site's staff nutritional experts, including pop-up e-mail forms that can be used to ask them questions.

What constitutes "rich" content. What customer hasn't misplaced a manual or lost an order form for maintenance or replacement parts? Your Web

Content

site can serve as an invaluable resource if you post in-depth information about products, services, company operations, executive profiles, and customer support.

The amount of content you put on the site depends on how much server space you want to pay for. Whether you rent or own server space, you must be sure to have enough redundant computing capacity to handle the additional content you are posting.

A good way to start is by posting information about the items that drive the top 20% of your sales, enabling customers to find information about the products that they want more frequently. Then you can measure requests for additional information and add Web pages as demand dictates. Because it costs so little—as little as $25 per page for a small-scale project—to post each additional page of information, there is every reason to post the routine material that you provide customers. Here are some examples of content that will enrich your site:

• *The basics, such as company mailing address, fax, and phone numbers.* You'll save your receptionist many time-consuming phone calls daily simply by adding this information at the bottom of your home page and on an official "Contact Us" page. If you have a toll-free customer service number, include it.

• *Directions to your physical location.* Deliverymen, visiting customers, prospects, and others who don't come to your office, store, or plant regularly will appreciate knowing how to find you. MapQuest offers free maps that can be placed on your site, either whole, on a page, or as a link to its site. MapQuest also offers a variety of enriched four-color maps, including a service that lets consumers plug in their starting point and your address, to get turn-by-turn directions. This is especially helpful for retailers, restaurant owners, and other businesses that have many first-time visitors or may have multiple locations. You can license the map software to reside on your own computer, or pay for a link to an interactive map hosted by MapQuest that is transparent to site visitors; that is, the directions appear to be coming directly from your site.

• *Company directory.* Customers can feel disconnected from you if their only option for sending e-mail is to an impersonal address such as "Webmaster," or, even worse, "customer support." Include pop-up e-mail forms with manager biographies so customers can connect to them directly. (Managers who fear becoming overwhelmed with e-mails can assign an administrative assistant to screen and route them to the appropriate departments.) At the very least, include a "real person" address for generic customer support so that customers don't feel that they are sending their e-mail into a void.

• *Product and service background information.* It may seem logical to group product descriptions together in one spot, but it's actually more helpful to customers to position it throughout your site with marketing copy. For instance, PurchasePro.com, a business services site, includes buttons linked to extensive service information clearly labeled "learn about it" and "get it done," for finding out more about its services, such as credit and direct mail fulfillment.

(Note: To access these buttons, look under "Business Resources" in the column on the right of PurchasePro.com's home page.)

• *Assembly directions and replacement parts.* Online replicas of the type of printed material usually packed with a product—e.g., warranties, product registration, a form for ordering replacement parts—are a time and labor saver for your customer service reps and for consumers who have lost or tossed the originals. For example, at a site operated by Armitage Hardware, a Chicago hardware store, consumers not only can get detailed technical specs about the outdoor barbecue grill model they may already have, but they also can buy replacement covers, grills, and other parts that wear out.

ROTOZIP SUPPLIES CUTTING-EDGE CONTENT

RotoZip Tool's Web site includes almost every customer service function imaginable—except the ability to make sales and take customers' money. The spiral-saw manufacturer leaves selling to the retailers that serve as its primary distribution channel—national home improvement chains and local hardware stores—and to its popular cable TV infomercials.

Through RotoZip's site, you can learn all about the company's sole product, the spiral saw, in all its variations. Visitors can get the lowdown on how to use various saw bits and "74 Spiral Saw Uses." They can also get answers to questions and swap ideas for spiral-saw projects with other spiral-saw fans. For prospective buyers, the site includes information on where RotoZip saws are sold as well as directions to the company's headquarters in Cross Plains, Wis.

The company has put nearly all of its marketing budget into pricey, but profitable, TV infomercials, leaving no money for advertising in other media, such as remodeling and home magazines. So the Web site is a crucial touchpoint for customers who want to find new uses for their spiral saws, explains Jason Kopras, executive vice president of RotoZip, and a member of the family that owns the company.

That's why Kopras has the site loaded with useful information that builds customer loyalty. For example, a condensed version of the owner's manual, highlighting critical safety information, is posted in English and Spanish. In-depth instructions for using specialty attachments are only a mouse-click away for handymen in the middle of a project. And, because the site directs users to local retailers, it has helped smooth any retailers' feathers that have been ruffled by the runaway success of the direct-sales infomercials.

Just the FAQs. The popular question-and-answer format was one of the first customer service tools adapted to Web sites—for good reason. This format is easily understood and reflects the actual questions that customers ask. This gives customers a sense that you're listening to them and responding. And, it's a format that is easily updated and expanded as your service reps track the questions that are asked often and then work with your Webmaster to post the answers.

Though it has enormous amounts of content, the Garden.com Web site offers a personalized service called the PlantFinder, which helps customers choose just the right plants for complete satisfaction. The site also featres a service called Garden Doctor, which posts customer queries in a searchable database. Seasonally related answers are listed on the Garden Doctor's main page. Besides previous answers, customers can also reach a "doctor" (an on-staff horticulturist) by toll-free phone and e-mail, with the caveat that it will take 24 hours to receive an answer.

You can leverage the friendly FAQ format even more by adding links to other parts of your Web site and useful links to other sites. Illustrator and publisher Mary Engelbreit's site, for instance, includes an enriched FAQ area that includes internal links. Visitors can link to the addresses and phone numbers of Engelbreit stores in malls as well as links to Internet storefronts featuring her home decorating items, dishes, watches, cards, books, calendars, and Christmas ornaments.

True to form. Forms are an inevitable part of business life. From product returns to reordering replacement parts to registering complaints, many customer-support functions require an accompanying form. You can make life easier for customers—and your employees—by providing forms on your site that customers can either fill out and submit online, or can print out and submit by fax or U.S. mail.

HOLIGAMES PLAYS WITH ONLINE ORDER FORM

It's unlikely that all of Syndi Kercher's customers will ever use her site to actually transact business. But, knowing them as she does, that's just fine with Kercher. By providing a printable order form that can be faxed or mailed to her, Kercher provides a way for customers to buy through the site without worrying about back-office technology or transactional security. Meanwhile, freed from the headaches of actually transacting business over the Internet, she concentrates on leveraging the site's value to her customers.

Kercher is president of Holigames, a Tucson company that makes and markets holiday-themed board games. Jewish history themes are the most popular so far, and those games are bought mainly by owners of neighborhood gift and religious supply shops. It's the ultimate mom-and-pop market, says Kercher. "A lot of [the shop owners] are older, not computer savvy, and they're reluctant to give out a credit-card number online," she says. "I take the risk of checks, because I know them so well. It's a religious audience, so my comfort level is higher."

As Kercher expands her line to include American history and other themes with broader appeal, however, she realizes that the number of credit-card orders are bound to rise. But as long as she can maintain close relationships with her customers, she's comfortable. After all, that's where she gets many of her best ideas for new products.

It's not difficult to train a staff member to mark up with HTML code a standard form originally created in a word processing program. Forms created in popular graphics programs, such as Adobe Illustrator and CorelDRAW, as well as those created in word processing formats, can be marked up by hand in HTML, or saved in HTML format, for easy posting to your Web site. Forms that customers fill out on your site and then send to designated people within your company can be forwarded to the database manager's queue so that the relevant information can be poured into the designated database format.

Complex and graphically attractive forms. More complex forms—legal documents, medical questionnaires, bills of lading and shipping, etc.—might require specialized formatting and graphic treatment. Adobe Acrobat's Portable Document Format (PDF) is popular software that enables these types of forms. The form is created in the Adobe format and posted as a downloadable form. However, customers also need to go to the Adobe Web site to download the software that interprets the form and enables it to pop up as intended. Adobe-formatted forms can't be opened through word processing formats. The Adobe enabling software is free, and many customers won't have any problems using it. Many will have downloaded and saved it on their hard drives already. For those customers who don't have Adobe's PDF, you'll need to provide a link to the Adobe site where they can download the software. You can also create forms in HTML format and recommend that customers open them as Web pages and then print them out. Still, it is smart to provide simplified, text-only versions of essential forms so that people who are averse to plug-ins don't have to bother with them.

Even sophisticated customers will occasionally have problems downloading forms and other graphically rich materials. Accompany your forms with a FAQ section that helps customers troubleshoot common problems, such as how to decompress compressed files. Perhaps because it is accustomed to dealing with confused users, the Internal Revenue Service site does an outstanding job of walking site visitors through potential complications of downloading forms. Click on the IRS's "Forms and Publications" section, www.irs.gov. It's worth checking out.

Posting a print catalog. Gooseberry Patch, a Delaware, Ohio, mail-order company that sells inexpensive country-themed kitchen and household tools and accessories, translated its homey print catalog to the Internet and started accepting orders online in 1999. Because the company gets basketsful of letters daily from customers sending compliments and submitting recipes for its popular cookbooks, company creative and operational teams wisely decided to develop a recipe exchange function on the site that engages customers in the same way. The "price of admission" into the recipe archive is the submission of another recipe.

Because Gooseberry's first Web site had been constructed using the database Lotus Notes and Lotus Script, Blue Cosmos Design, the Web consulting firm Gooseberry Patch chose to create the Web version of its catalog, stuck with that format for the expanded, transactional site. Site visitors can scroll through a list of items that cost $25 or less—an experience similar to leafing through the catalog; or, go right to the cookbook selection; or, search for items by catalog number, theme, and price. The strategy worked; the site garnered $500,000 in sales in its debut season.

John Ray, Blue Cosmos IT director, says that other databases that work at least as well for catalogs include the Linux-based PostgreSQL, Oracle 8I, and Microsoft's SQL Server 7.0.

The process involves entering of each product picture and description, creating a searchable database. Listing subcategories in the search menus provides useful landmarks so visitors can quickly look up a specific item. Keeping the item names, stock numbers, technical information, and categories identical to your printed catalogs not only makes it much easier to transfer the information into the electronic format and minimize data conversion tasks, but also enables long-time customers to search by stock numbers and other shortcuts that they may have developed on their own.

However, if you have a very small array of products to display and don't need an interactive catalog with search functions, you can use a Web publishing program, such as those offered by Adobe and Corel, to create Web pages with digital pictures and item descriptions. Simply list the names of the items alphabetically or group them in categories.

Bulletin boards and meeting places. Many companies count customers among their best customer-support resources. Enthusiastic, well-informed customers who are glad to share ideas, information, and inspiration with other customers often welcome the chance to do so through bulletin boards and message centers at your site. In the process, the interchange, which can be read by all, adds content to your site.

Bulletin boards allow customers to ask and answer each other's questions in a text format, with the threads of conversation appearing in successively indented paragraphs. Any customer can drop in and see all the pre-

Content

TIP Don't underestimate the legal implications of bulletin boards or the amount of maintenance they require. You'll need to appoint a bulletin board administrator who scans the comments posted to the board at least daily to delete potentially libelous or embarrassing comments. To minimize the housekeeping chores associated with a board, choose software that allows you to set up protocols that ban certain words, or even certain misbehaving users.

ceding discussions and comments. You can also archive useful discussions for future reference by customers.

Companies such as Netbula, produce bulletin-board software that runs on commonly used e-commerce platforms. Netbula's AnyBoard, for example, requires the popular CGI protocol and uses Perl 5 programming language. Bulletin and message boards are installed in tandem with the rest of your Web site as an operating subsystem.

Real-time meetings as well as real-time chat can showcase your in-house experts and authoritative customers. For instance, a cadre of customers may want to know more about the technology underlying a particular new product. Setting up a real-time meeting online is an efficient way to get your research and development staff "together" with the customers for a casual discussion. Koz.com produces a popular software suite, ichat, which supports bulletin boards and real-time meeting places.

Useful links. Links to other Web sites can be of enormous service to customers, and by association, they increase the content available through your site. Because the links you post carry an implied endorsement, carefully check out each link and the authorities behind it. Be sure to include only links that provide genuine value to customers. As follow up, assign a staffer to revisit those sites regularly to see how they are changing.

"CHAT" GETS DOWN TO EXPERTISE

Expectations about bulletin boards and chats sometimes run too high. For example, when chat rooms and message boards started to become centers of passionate customer interaction, Daniel Harrison, president of Poolandspa.com, a Long Island, N.Y., pool and hot-tub supply company, thought an online community would also work for him. So he paid $2,500 for the software, and his ISP installed the technology on his site. Harrison promoted the new community on the site's main pages and offered a 10% discount on all products bought during a scheduled live online chat. But at the appointed hour, just 10 people came to the party. Undaunted, Harrison figured it was just a matter of time. However, the next scheduled live chat yielded only six people.

The company was receiving "a tremendous amount" of e-mail from customers, says Harrison, so he thought he could translate e-mail to chat. Always willing to try the next new technology, Harrison says he followed the AOL model for chat, but without one key ingredient. AOL featured celebrity hosts—a big draw. He was trying to make an event out of something with far less glamour. And he wasn't meeting his customers' needs.

"If the hot-tub water is turning your kid's hair green, you don't want to wait for the answer until [the live chat at] Wednesday night at 10," he quips. "My customers don't want to talk to each other. If they have a question, they want to talk to an expert."

Poolandspa.com still offers online visitors the opportunity to chat, but Harrison now understands the role of a chat on his site. It has been useful, he says, for customer interaction and customer recommendations about Poolandspa.com's products and their use.

Checking order status. Even if they have not actually ordered something through your site, customers may expect useful content from your site, such as getting the status of their orders by e-mailing you. This is one of the most direct examples of customers' querying a Web site for information. They may want to know when a back-ordered item will be available or when a large item arriving via freight is likely to be delivered. An "order status" page that includes a pop-up e-mail box that directs e-mail inquiries to the person in customer service who tracks order status will help your employees respond to customers.

This assumes, of course, that your internal network enables service reps to link into your distribution and shipping systems so they can find out where the customer's order is. Basic inventory management software is included in popular small-business accounting software such as Intuit's QuickBooks. Specialized inventory and shipping software that dovetails with popular database programs is relatively inexpensive; Skandata's Skantrak inventory processing system costs approximately $1,500 for a small-business site license. You can also arrange with United Parcel Service and FedEx to place their order tracking service on your site. You can have it appear as a box in which customers enter the order tracking

TIP You can leverage your links by participating in link exchanges, such as LinkExchange or SmartAge, in which a broker company aggregates banner ads created by small companies and places the ads on sites with similar content. This may enhance your customer service if your site ends up with links that are complementary to yours. There is a caveat, however: because you can't control the types of links that land on your site, it could also confuse customers.

number and the status pops up, or you can simply place a link so customers can plug in the tracking numbers at the shippers' sites.

A Web site rich with useful information and feedback tools yields valuable insights about what kind of information customers find helpful, what formats they prefer for receiving that information, and how technically sophisticated they are. The more comfortable customers are with your Web site and your staff's prompt response to their inquiries, the more your customers will know and trust your company. This is a valuable retention tool, but it also paves the way for successful customer support of online purchasing, the subject of the next chapter. ■

COMPANIES AND SITES IN THIS CHAPTER

Adobe Systems **www.adobe.com**

Armitage Hardware **www.webergrills.com**

Blue Cosmos Design **www.bluecosmos.com**

Corel **www.corel.com**

Mary Engelbreit Studios
www.maryengelbreit.com

FedEx **www.fedex.com**

Garden.com **www.garden.com**

Gooseberry Patch **www.gooseberrypatch.com**

Holigames **www.holigames.com**

Internal Revenue Service **www.irs.gov**

Koz.com **www.koz.com**

MapQuest **www.mapquest.com**

Microsoft **www.microsoft.com**

Netbula **www.netbula.com**

Oracle **www.oracle.com**

Poolandspa.com **www.poolandspa.com**

Postgre SQL **www.postgresql.org**

PurchasePro **www.purchasepro.com**

QuickBooks **www.quickbooks.com**

RotoZip Tool **www.rotozip.com**

Skandata **www.skandata.com**

SmartAge **www.smartage.com**

United Parcel Service **www.ups.com**

Vitamins.com **www.vitamins.com**

Jennifer White **www.worklessmakemore.com**

Content

Chapter 5

Real-time Contact

The first critical point in customer service is, literally, the point of purchase—when the customer is about to buy, but may need a little more information or reassurance before taking the plunge. Technologies that range from the familiar (toll-free phone lines) to the cutting edge (voice over Internet) enable customer support representatives to offer real-time help that can ease customers over the decision threshold and into a purchase.

Help via phone. When they have questions, most customers naturally reach for the telephone. To support that tendency your main phone number should be prominently displayed on your home page and throughout your site. Personal Creations, a site that offers personalized merchandise, such as picture frames and blankets, does a thorough job of making sure customers can contact a service rep at every turn. Its toll-free number is displayed at the bottom of most of the company's Web pages, especially the home page and product description pages. A prominent "Help" button on the home page zips customers to a page that offers several options for support—phone, e-mail, order status, offline ordering options, and FAQs.

Of course, customer support staff who answer the phone must have instant access to the current version of your Web site so they can see the same pages that customers are referring to. Even before updates—such as clearance items that are suddenly sold out—are posted, service people need to know about them. One way to accomplish this is to have the staff that maintains your site send instant messages to your call center staffers.

The reps who field questions from online customers will need to refer to all promotional offers currently in effect—whether the offers are made through general advertising, partnerships with other Web sites, or through "specials" for your online customers only. One effective way to keep your reps in the loop is to have your marketing staff maintain a list of current specials and promotions in a small database that the reps can tap into.

Your call-center staff must also have access to the customer profile database so they can tailor their responses to the customer's prior preferences and buying patterns.

Managers of companies that sell over the Web report that customers often call to ask a question and then figure, "While I've got you on the phone, I might as well place my order." Reps need to be attuned to customers' hints and be prepared to close the sale.

Instant messaging. Many Web users, especially teenagers, love instant messaging. This technology resides on your Web site and "recognizes" visitors who have a compatible instant messaging system. Visitors can check to see if you're online and, if so, willing to converse with them. If you are, a box pops up, and each types in comments to the other and sends them back and forth instantly. Because so many people are comfortable with instant messaging, it has wide appeal. If your customer service reps are willing to drop everything to respond to an instant message, they will be giving customers the most immediate help possible.

In its current state of evolution, instant messaging (IM) has two significant drawbacks. First, there are several competing protocols, or sets of technnical specifications, and they aren't compatible. Two of the most popular are ICQ, and America Online Instant Messenger (AIM). If you've equipped your site with AIM, visitors who "speak in ICQ" can't communicate with you via instant messaging. This means you have to recruit customers to the protocol you've chosen. It also means constantly directing customers to the Web site of the IM protocol you've chosen. Still, IM is a powerful tool if you want to capture impulse sales by answering shoppers' questions immediately. If you are willing to make sure that an employee or customer service

BOB CHINN'S CRABS DANCE TO THE BEAT OF THE NET

Bob Chinn's Crab House, a sprawling restaurant in Wheeling, Ill., dishes up crab by the bushel and mai tais by the gallon to a million people every year. It's a party kind of place, and the restaurant's Web site—with its motif of shimmying crustaceans—reflects that.

Thanks to its site, Bob Chinn's is extending its brand far beyond the Chicago area and building a national mail-order business in the process. For its overnight seafood deliveries to retail customers, however, general manager Frank D'Angelo wants customers to call rather than place orders online. They can purchase gift certificates online, but even then, Chinn's calls each customer back for verification. Unlike the fill-in-and-send order form for gift certificates, there is no order form on the site for overnight deliveries of seafood.

Customers call and talk with the receptionist (Chinn's only customer service rep) because seafood availability is so erratic and consumers' expectations are so high. D'Angelo wants customers to have an extra level of reassurance about how the seafood is packed, shipped, and when and where it will arrive so they can open and refrigerate it immediately. The receptionist processes the online order through the same payment system used by the restaurant's waitstaff. The order is printed out and trotted over to the packing crew in the chilled storage area, where it is assembled and sent on its way.

D'Angelo cooked up the overnight express service for the holidays, in December 1998, and it resulted in 64 orders. In 1999, that mushroomed to 600. Considering the 1999 season a test, Chinn's management is applying what it learned then to smooth out back-office functions for an expected tenfold increase in volume for Christmas 2000.

rep is always ready for such interruptions, it is an inexpensive, customer-friendly tool for providing real-time help.

Real-time chat. Chat is very similar to instant messaging, but with one important caveat: Both parties are situated on the same Web page, typing comments into adjacent boxes, instead of zapping messages from one point on the Internet to another, as is possible with instant messaging. Chat is superior to IM in that it resides permanently on your Web site, enabling customers to get help the moment they need it through your service reps. Instant messaging forces you to be more reactive—answering questions when they pop up on your screen out of nowhere—and also leaves customers wondering how they'll get their questions answered if they're online, but you're not.

TIP Teenagers are the heaviest users of instant messaging. If you are marketing to teens and college students, instant messaging can be a "cool" signal that you're part of their world. However, other customers, may shy away from instant messaging because they think you're targeting only teens.

Typically, chat is indicated by a "Live Help" button situated on the home page and displayed prominently at various points where customers are likely to make decisions—such as clothing size charts and throughout the checkout process. Coldwater Creek, a catalog and online merchant of women's clothing, does a great job of introducing its chat function. The "Instant Help" button, located on the top toolbar, floats above every page. When customers click on the button, a box pops up for their comments, accompanied by an introduction to the service: "Simply enter your question, concern, or comment in the field below. Within moments, a customer service representative will respond in the adjacent box. To continue your conversation, simply send

> **TIP** Ensure that the instant messaging (IM) or real-time chat technology that you're considering has a function that enables you to save the exchanges for later review. Archived IM conversations can be reviewed to determine what types of questions customers ask, how prepared your service reps are to answer them, and if you need to conduct specialized training for your reps to further leverage the potential of instant messaging and real-time chat.

another question or comment."

Questions scroll off the screen as new script is typed in, allowing both parties to keep track of the dialogue. Skilled customer service reps can attend to as many as two chats and four e-mails at a time—while also calling up information about customers and orders.

The great advantage of instant messaging and chat is that the entire interaction takes place on the computer—a boon to the majority of consumers, who have only one phone line at home. After all, if someone is already using his phone line to go online, he can't also be talking on the phone asking questions. Instant messaging and chat solve this problem.

Software vendors that produce chat technology typically also offer a whole menu of related Internet customer service technology, such as page pushing and voice-over-Internet (both described below). Popular vendors include PeopleLink, CosmoCom, PeopleSupport, and PSINet.

Personalization. A variation of live chat is personalization—for example, having reps welcome repeat customers personally through online chat. This can be accomplished with a combination of cookies that your site leaves on your customers' computers, customers' self-identification when they log in or register, and your reps' rapid access to your customer database. Think of these online hellos as the virtual version of a store greeter. The greeter's welcome may simply pop up in a text box, accompanied by an offer to assist the shopper.

Jeff Gaus, vice president of marketing for ITXC (formerly eFusion), an e-commerce customer service solutions firm, recommends having service reps make special incentives or offers to high-volume or high-revenue customers based on their profitability to your company. "That conveys your investment in the customer," he says. The welcome and offers can be made through whatever means the customer prefers—chat, messaging, or voice.

You can achieve a similar effect by using cookies and linking your customer preferences database to your site. When a repeat customer logs on, an automated personalized text greeting can pop up. Amazon.com, for instance, is famous for these personalized greetings, which often include recommendations for new books, CDs, auctions, and other items tailored to the customer's prior purchases.

While greetings can be friendly, customers can also perceive them as being intrusive—especially if the customer is worried about privacy issues and the greeting includes information that seems a tad too intimate. Signal respect for customers' privacy concerns by asking them to quickly sign in when they arrive. Once they've made the effort to signal their presence, they will be more comfortable if personalized greetings pop up. These may suggest, for example, that they look at a new line of bathroom towels that comes in the same colors as bedsheets they bought the month before.

Page pushing. In response to a phone or live chat request, service reps can force a relevant page to pop up on the shopper's computer screen. This is most helpful if the customer is hopelessly lost on the site, groping for a particular item, or if the information the customer seeks is rarely accessed (such as a technical diagram). When reps have immediate access to databases of directions, diagrams, product specs, and other materials, they simply find the right item and drop it in front of the customer on the computer screen. This is a great way to make rarely-asked-for documents available to customers through your site, without having to figure out a way to permanently store them on the site.

The "push" comes through a channel temporarily created between your company's computer and the customer's, using tools such as Marimba's Castanet or Microsoft's Active Channels. Of course, the pages being pushed must be in HTML format so that they'll be recognized by the customer's

JEWELRY SALES CLICK WITH PART-TIME CHAT

The Internet never sleeps. Does that mean that your customer service reps can't, either? It depends on the type of product you're selling. For huge, retailers whose call centers are already taking orders round-the-clock, it isn't much of a stretch to add online chat and prompt e-mail responses in the wee hours.

However, customer relationship experts say that consumers don't have the same expectations for small specialty businesses. In fact, the more specialized your offerings, the more likely people are to be patient when contacting your staff experts. That means if you're offering very specialized, expert information, you probably have plenty of leeway in the type and amount of access you provide to knowledgeable customer service reps.

Mondera, an online retailer of diamonds and fine jewelry in New York City, was well aware that few customers would plunk down thousands of dollars for a diamond ring or bracelet without first calling the company, even if their only motivation was to make sure that there's a real company behind the Web site. Because gifts of jewelry are often made for once-in-browser. If the page being pushed is to include interactive material, such as hyperlinks, it must be formatted in JavaScript or a similarly powerful Web authoring program. That's not a problem for pages that are already formatted for your site, but if service reps are delving into archived material to push it to customers' screens, they will need to know how to quickly convert the material to a Web-compatible format.

Page pushing is especially helpful to shoppers who have become disoriented on a site—for instance, they want to retrace their steps and find an item they saw earlier, but can't locate. Recently, a Mondera.com shopper

a-lifetime occasions and because they are expensive, management wanted to make sure that Mondera customers not only got lots of details about carats and cuts, but also that the service reps understood the emotional implications of the purchase. In short, they have to be knowledgeable and sympathetic.

Experienced gemologists, of course, aren't necessarily trained in customer service, so Mondera spends time prepping them before making them available to customers from 9:00 a.m. to 8:00 p.m. daily. Most customers take several days to mull over their choice of fine jewelry, so Mondera isn't losing any spur-of-the-moment sales to insomniacs who must talk to a gemologist at 3:00 a.m.

Besides, as experience shows, people would rather take their time with the gemologist—to thoroughly understand the setting, how their piece of jewelry is being created, the customized options, and details of delivery—rather than zip through the order and end up proposing with an engagement ring that's a couple of carats shy of impressive.

wanted to compare two antique bracelets with diamonds of unusual cuts and got stuck in a cul-de-sac of definitions of gemstone styles. After a short real-time chat with a service rep, in which the shopper gave a general description of the lost page with the bracelet she was considering, the rep found the page and made it pop up on the shopper's screen.

Voice-over-Internet. Software manufacturers are working hard to funnel live voice interaction over Internet lines so that consumers can click on a button and carry on live conversations with reps through the sound card embedded in their computers. The jury's still out on this one. Some e-commerce consultants say that natural conversation is the easiest way to help customers, while others find the experience of talking to a disembodied voice disconcerting. Live chat is much less intimidating because so many people are comfortable with e-mail, which has some obvious similarities to chat.

JavaScript applets—tiny programs or "cookies"—embedded on a customer's own computer pave the way for voice-over-Internet by creating a minuscule "channel" for the software containing the voice stream from your computer to your customer's computer. The enabling software compresses the voice stream through relatively slow (i.e., 56K) Internet connections so that it is almost as smooth as voice over telephone, although the transmission quality depends a lot on the speed of the two modems and on "potholes" on the Internet.

To avoid distracting lags in transmission, customers must have relatively up-to-date computer systems, such as Windows 95, in order to accept voice-over-Internet. And, they must have functional speakers on their computers. The software that supports voice on the customer service side requires a great deal of memory (one popular program, eShare's NetAgent, demands 100 MB of storage and a bare minimum of 128 RAM). If you're using voice frequently, you may have to upgrade the speed of your Internet connections and add memory to accommodate this function. That's especially important if you find your customers like the voice support and you start recording frequently asked questions and saving other voice files for frequent use. A good way to experiment with voice-over-Internet is to use the live demos at companies that offer the service, such as Lipstream Networks.

One great advantage that chat and e-mail customer service tools have over voice is that they are easily archived and searched. That's hard to do with voice; you may not be able to review customer support sessions as easily, and thus lose the chance to see what strategies best help customers and where your reps need more training.

Training customer support staff. Because customers may be unfamiliar with technologies such as live chat, voice-over-Internet, and page pushing, your service reps must have a thorough understanding of how to introduce these technologies to customers. They can't assume that the customer they're helping knows what to expect when he or she clicks on the "Live Help Now" button. Customers may be startled, not sure how to proceed, and confused as to how much help the rep can actually provide through chat, page pushing, or voice-over-Internet.

One surefire way to help your service reps understand customers' potential problems is to have them shop at other Web sites. They'll see the many variations on the plain vanilla theme of checking out, and how many unexpected, unexplainable technological glitches can thwart a successful sale or communication. This will help them understand the causes of customer confusion.

Coaching customers through unfamiliar technology, however, may be new to your reps. They should develop a sixth sense about customers' ability to manipulate cache refresh screens, track through a Web site, adjust their screens to see an entire site at once, and other often-overlooked technical details. This will entail technical training from your Web site staff,

Webmaster, or online agency in how to explain technical elements. Companies such as Impact Learning Systems International and the Service Quality Institute offer programs and consulting services that can help employees master new technologies and techniques.

Changing with technology. As you prepare to expand your online transactional capacity, review the options offered by the e-commerce software you

CLOSING THE GAP BETWEEN VIRTUAL AND ACTUAL

Bob Curry, founder and chief operating officer of HomeTownStores.com, an online home and garden store, was challenged to bridge the gap between virtual and actual when his site outstripped his wildest expectations. HomeTownStores started out as the online version of the hardware stores that Curry runs in his hometown of Quincy, Mass. In early 1998, his son, Sean, pushed him to set up shop online. Curry never was under the delusion that he could raid the store's inventory to satisfy online orders. His first order of business was to set up an arrangement with a Memphis distributor so that completed orders are automatically forwarded there for picking, packing, and shipping.

The thing that nagged at Curry was how to replicate online the actual experience of stopping by his store. "We learned through the bricks-and-mortar business how important it is to connect with customers. We give away free popcorn all day in the store. How do we bring that to the Web?" he asks. "We didn't think it would be a people business. We thought we could handle it in a generic way with templates, and that's not true. The sites that are successful are those that respond when you ask a question."

Before long, HomeTownStores was getting a tidal wave of up to have been relying on so far. Software developers are always introducing more powerful, richer products. Even if your transactional test lasted only for a few months, new software may have been introduced in the meantime that is a much better fit for your debut into full-time online customer support.

That's what executives at Medical SelfCare in Emeryville, Calif., learned as they ramped up their site (SelfCare.com) throughout 1999. The company

1,000 e-mails a day, requesting information about how to use particular products or the name of that "ball thing" in the toilet tank. Curry's staff was going nuts serving both real and virtual customers. So he brought in a virtual customer service firm called icontact.com (now heyinc.com). Its customer service reps are linked to the HomeTownStores servers, so they have the same database information about products and other details as the hardware store employees. icontact reps introduce themselves to new arrivals to HomeTownStores via live chat, offering to answer questions and help shoppers find what they're looking for. Only questions that can't be answered through the store's online library of reference material are forwarded to the seasoned store clerks. That amounts to about 50 e-mails a day, divided among several staffers—a reasonable volume.

Now, Curry is tracking and archiving the frequently asked questions to put even more resources at customers' finger tips. He also hopes to start setting up online chats with featured store employees to establish the site as the best place on the Web for real-life answers about home and garden issues.

And Curry hasn't forgotten the personal touch. HomeTownStore reps make hundreds of phone calls monthly to make sure that orders arrived, to solve any problems, and to just say thanks.

was founded in 1976 as an educational health and wellness magazine. A few years later, the magazine evolved into a direct-mail catalog business specializing in products that help customers stay healthy and fit. John Kendig, vice-president of merchandising, and Andrea Alfano, vice-president of marketing, say that their biggest concern was not how to deliver good customer service, but how to translate their already successful techniques to the Internet.

It pays to go interactive. Their first foray was a site that simply mirrored the catalog. It went live at the end of 1998. Based partly on the types of questions that customers asked and the words they plugged into the site's internal search engine, SelfCare's managers started mapping out a broader, more interactive site. First, they negotiated with several respected health magazines and general content syndicators to buy the rights to post articles about medical breakthroughs and new treatments. They also added interactive tools, such as a step-by-step questionnaire that helps visitors figure out what type of weight-loss diet might be most successful for them. Customers can register to get regular e-mail reminders to perform their monthly breast exams. By mid-2000, more than 100,000 customers (mainly women) were logged in the SelfCare database, and more than 15,000 had signed up for some sort of e-mail service or specialty newsletter.

The expanded site also enabled SelfCare.com to offer products that aren't in the company's catalog, not to mention special sales and clearance items. A priority was to make sure that customers' e-mails are answered in two hours or less. The company manages its e-mail with Kana Communications's automated e-mail software and handles phone inquiries through Lucent's Definity Prologix system with CentreVu CMS/ACD functions that enable customers traversing the site to click a button and engage in instant messaging back and forth with a customer service rep.

SelfCare also added real-time, online response mechanisms developed by LivePerson. When real-time chat was installed on the site, the company brought its call center in-house and cross-trained its platoon of 20 customer service reps in the chat function.

"If you have someone who's good at customer service, it's not that much different to handle [questions] by phone or live chat," notes Kendig. "We've found that the important thing is to have the reps trained well to handle a customer through any channel, from e-mail to phone and live chat."

SelfCare also has three staffers who do nothing but test products and keep up with preventive-care health trends and news. They are situated adjacent to the customer service reps so they can confer with them about a question or even get online or on the phone with a customer directly.

Of course, customers also expect to get their orders from SelfCare promptly. How to use technology to accelerate your fulfillment operations is the subject of the next chapter. ∎

Real-time Contact

COMPANIES AND SITES IN THIS CHAPTER

America Online. www.aol.com

Bob Chinn's Crab House www.bobchinns.com

Coldwater Creek www.coldwatercreek.com

CosmoCom www.cosmocom.com

eShare Communications www.eshare.com

HomeTownStores.com www.hometownstores.com

icontact.com (!hey inc.) www.heyinc.com

ICQ www.icq.com

Impact Learning Systems International
www.impactlearning.com

ITXC www.itxc.com

Java and Java Script (Sun Microsystems)
www.java.sun.com/index.html

Kana Communications www.kana.com

Lipstream Networks www.lipstream.com

LivePerson www.liveperson.com

Lucent Technologies www.lucent.com

Marimba www.marimba.com

Microsoft www.microsoft.com

Mondera www.mondera.com

PeopleLink www.peoplelink.com

Personal Creations www.personalize.com

PSINet www.psinet.com

SelfCare (Medical SelfCare) www.selfcare.com

Service Quality Institute
www.customer-service.com

Chapter 6

Fulfillment: Betting on the Back Office

Robert M. Klare, vice-president of sales for FASCOR, an inventory and ful-fillment software firm in Cincinnati, works with online retailers large and small. He has one piece of advice for managers of e-commerce sites: Make sure that your back-office operations are streamlined so that cus-tomers are fully informed at all times about exactly what you have in stock and how soon they can expect to get their hands on it. "If you run over the last box of games with your forklift, the Web site needs to know that there are no more," says Klare.

In 2000, e-commerce technology providers started including fulfillment functions in their software offerings. Once an order is completed through your Web site, it can be sent electronically or manually to your warehouse, with the order information forwarded to your accounting department. New technology smoothes the path of packing and shipping orders and even of accepting returns. As an alternative, a new generation of suppliers is crop-ping up to handle the entire chore on an outsourced basis.

As a compromise between do-it-yourself and outsourcing fulfillment, also consider relying on carrier expertise. With e-commerce exploding in 2000, huge shippers, such as UPS and FedEx, realized that small and mid-size companies could use help with tracking, packing, labeling, and ship-ping. Thus, both now offer fulfillment services geared to the Internet.

Your capability. As orders roll in from your Web site, vital information must be forwarded to several internal departments. Items must be deduct-ed from inventory; the shipping department needs to check each order to be sure that it's packed and shipped as requested, and accounting must be noti-fied for billing purposes. If your order volume is relatively light, you may not need to automate the entire process. Standard small-business software, such as Intuit's QuickBooksPro, has an inventory function for inputting details about new inventory. Sales data can be copied from the order forms and pasted where appropriate to various sections of QuickBooksPro, including its built-in shipping and label generation form. It is inefficient to copy and re-enter some information, but if you are only shipping a few items weekly, the cost and effort to install a full-bore, integrated e-commerce system probably is not worth it.

As online sales volume grows, it will start to strain your small-scale fulfillment solutions. Here are several warning signs that you need to invest in specialized inventory management and fulfillment software:

- *Order fulfillment delays are steadily lengthening.*
- *Employees not normally involved in fulfillment are pulled in.*
- *Warehouse and fulfillment staff are routinely caught by surprise. They must scramble to order more stock and procure more shipping supplies.*

Fulfillment software. Many e-commerce software packages include integrated fulfillment reporting, labeling, and other functions. For example, software from OpenOrders, a Newton, Mass., developer, enables businesses to add fulfillment components as needed. Oracle offers iStore, iPayment, and iSupport packages that automatically update every transaction throughout the system. Customer service reps, for instance, can check inventory levels through the iSupport component, ensuring that the order can be processed smoothly. One great advantage of integrated systems is that they support numerous reports and enable managers to find out exactly what is happening at any point in the order process.

Making the transition from a familiar but inefficient order fulfillment system requires patience, but can pay off generously. One toy distributor found that, at the end of a three-month fulfillment improvement project, the total time it took to fill an order from the moment credit-card payment cleared to packing had been reduced from an hour to six minutes.

Should you outsource? Declan Dunn hit a gold mine in 1996 when he formed ADNetInternational.com, an Internet marketing firm in Chico, Calif. At that time, everyone from mom-and-pops to multinationals were trying to figure out how to integrate the Internet into their marketing plans. Dunn and his partner, Patrick Anderson, had enough answers to launch a consulting firm. And as consultants, the partners started churning out books, manuals, and audio tapes.

At first, the pair's wives got stuck with the chore of collecting orders that were faxed and e-mailed in, entering them into Quicken accounting software and schlepping the orders to the post office. That rapidly wore thin. As the company grew, fulfillment was delegated to an office manager, who negotiated deals with local printers and tape duplicators for hundreds of copies at a time. That saved money, but ADNet's staffers began tripping over inventory piled in the firm's corridors. And the office manager still spent hours every week downloading orders from the secure server, importing them into Filemaker Pro, generating labels, exporting the customer file data into Quicken, and then making sure that the credit-card payments had cleared, before trekking to the post office.

Finally, Dunn and Anderson had had enough. They installed an e-commerce system with customized affiliate software at ActiveMarketplace.com, which cut down on the manual processing but still left the shipping problem. The shipping dilemma was solved by iFulfill.com, a Dundee, Mich., firm set up specifically to process transactions and fulfillment for dotcoms. iFulfill president Paul Purdue says it takes only three minutes to download orders from subscribing companies' sites, pick and pack them, and update the companies' records. Fees for the service are on a sliding scale; the first order costs $4; 50 or more per month, $1 each. iFulfill also takes a 7% cut of each credit-card transaction it processes.

In addition, Purdue also arranged with the local Kinko's in Dundee to electronically store ActiveMarketplace's books and print them as needed. Short runs are printed whenever stock at the iFulfill warehouse runs low.

SIZING UP FULFILLMENT OPTIONS

In-house

Advantages
- Complete control
- Ability to react quickly to problems
- Relatively easy to control costs

Disdvantages
- Difficult to attract and keep staff
- Difficult to accommodate seasonal rushes
- Capital tied up in non-revenue-producing assets, such as packing materials and space

Outsource

Advantages
- Frees up space by storing inventory, including packaging, elsewhere
- Relief from daily noise and shuffle of shipping
- May not have to invest in software
- Flexibility (can use several regional fulfillment houses)

Disadvantages
- Difficult to monitor quality of packaging and condition of goods shipped
- May require long-term contract
- Can be expensive
- May not use software compatible with your system
- May not accommodate special requests, such as gift-wrapping service

Fulfillment

These are delivered directly to iFulfill. Dunn and Anderson simply forward a fresh file whenever they update a book. ActiveMarketplace's tape duplicators agreed to a similar arrangement.

When customers hit "Send" at the ActiveMarketplace site, their orders go directly to iFulfill. The outsource firm regularly generates reports, including customer database updates and analyses of average order size and what items tend to be purchased together. Best of all, from ADNet's viewpoint,

Fulfillment

GARDEN.COM GROWS A FULFILLMENT MODEL

With its clever graphics, in-depth content, and customized service tools, Garden.com, an Austin, Tex., company, has become a perennial favorite with people who get their hands dirty for fun. It was developed from the ground up with an extensive network of suppliers, including local nurseries, geared to provide customers around the country with live plants for their gardens. (A few non-perishable products, such as gloves and books, are shipped directly from Garden.com's warehouse.)

Garden.com has become a model of fulfillment efficiency. TRELLIS, the company's virtual supply-chain system, coordinates the shipments of its gardening products through the national network. Once an order is set in motion, payment is processed through Garden.com's site, and then immediately forwarded to one of the site's 70-plus local suppliers for fulfillment. The company uses prepackaged software systems that include Kana Communications's automated e-mail software to send customers real-time messages regarding the status of their orders. Garden.com also uses eShare's interface, which allows a customer-solutions representative to provide live online help at the time of the order.

everything happens off-site, so the company can focus on growing its core business without shipping distractions.

Volume discounts. A big push in orders may allow you to gain volume discounts from your outsourced fulfillment house, or to get additional discounts from materials suppliers and shippers. For example, Copera, a White Plains, N.Y., firm that specializes in handling back-office fulfillment for Web companies, charges a minimum of 20¢ per transaction to process credit-card orders for customers that use it for $15,000 or less in sales annually. The rate drops as a client's volume increases. As fulfillment outsourcers proliferate, many will offer special deals to gain customers. ZeeTech Shipping Fulfillment, for example, doesn't charge for receiving or stocking merchandise, while Quality Fulfillment Services, touts its ability to integrate its software with its customers' at various points along the order processing route.

Ultimate fulfillment: Same-day delivery. Same-day service? If you think your company is too small or doesn't have the resources, consider how a New York gift shop makes good on its "same-day" promise. Farrel Miller, co-founder of Giftworld.com, a Manhattan-based online gift store, knew that he had to find a way to distinguish his shop from all the other Web sites selling gifts. He partnered with a small chain of gift shops that had the capability to offer same-day delivery in selected cities. Miller spread the word about the partnership arrangement while turning fulfillment into a distinguishing characteristic for Giftworld.com.

"As a typical guy, I wait until the 'day-of' to get gifts," says Miller, who believes that Giftworld's same-day delivery option truly sets his site apart. "A lot of people think of gift time only when it hits the calendar, so the immediacy of delivery is a very compelling factor."

As he was setting up the site in mid-1999, Miller set out to find partners in key metropolitan markets that shared his perspective. He teamed up with

Chiasso, a Chicago-based chain of gift, arts, and crafts stores. Executives at both companies agreed on an array of about 100 items to keep in stock at Chiasso at all time, drawn from both companies' perennial best-sellers.

Then, Miller lined up a national courier service to make the Giftworld.com deliveries the backbone of its daily schedule. Same-day orders that arrive at Giftworld.com by 1:00 p.m. (EST) are grouped for electronic transmission to the appropriate Chiasso stores. Chiasso employees pick and pack the orders, handling details such as gift wrap and personalized notes. The courier service arrives at each Chiasso store at 2:30 p.m. local time and whisks away the packages for delivery by 6:00 p.m. to businesses and 10:00 p.m. to homes.

So far, same-day delivery favorites are executive gifts, such as the massage pen, travel accessories, and gourmet food baskets. And, Miller's hunch has paid off: Same-day service now accounts for more than 15% of all orders.

Efficient fulfillment and delivery reinforce customers' trust in your company, and satisfied customers tend to reward you with repeat sales and referrals. But there are other rewards, too. Online sales create important data. Summary reports and other tracking tools to quantify the success of your customer service efforts are the subject of the next chapter. ∎

COMPANIES AND SITES IN THIS CHAPTER

ActiveMarketplace (ADNet) **www.activemarketplace.com**

Copera **www.copera.com**

eShare Technologies **www.eshare.com**

FASCOR **www.fascor.com**

Garden.com **www.garden.com**

Giftworld.com **www.giftworld.com**

iFulfill.com **www.ifulfill.com**

Kana Communications **www.kana.com**

Kinko's **www.kinkos.com**

OpenOrders **www.openorders.com**

Oracle **www.oracle.com**

Quality Fulfillment Services **www.qfsinc.com**

QuickBooksPro **www.quickbooks.com**

ZeeTech Shipping Fulfillment **www.zeetech-shipping.com**

Chapter 7

Tracking the Return

Serving customers through the Internet can be highly effective, but it's not cheap in terms of time, effort, or money. It's important to track precisely the results you get from Internet-based CRM so that you can quickly modify the online tools that aren't capturing sales or customer loyalty.

Because you already have some type of an off-line customer service, it's relatively easy to detect the difference when you add Internet-based CRM. And the very nature of database-driven Net tools means that you can capture vast amounts of details into your database and slice that information many ways. Early indications from numerous e-commerce research firms are encouraging. Surveys show that the more comfortable consumers become with the Internet and e-commerce, the more they spend online.

Pinpointing the real paybacks. According to an April 2000 study by ActivMedia, cyber-shoppers who have been online for five years or more spend more than twice as much (an average of $388 per transaction) as those who have been online only a year (average: only $187 per transaction). So you have a good chance of gaining even more loyalty and resulting sales, as you strive to deliver excellent online customer service.

To measure the results of your online CRM efforts, first determine the key indicators you want to track. These might include:

- *Time*. The amount of time customers spend on the site before buying
- *Abandoned carts*. The number of shopping carts that are abandoned midway through the purchasing process
- *Last Web pages*. The last pages that customers view before they exit
- *First purchase*. The average amount spent on first purchases
- *Subsequent purchases*. The average amount that customers spend on subsequent purchases

• *Opt in.* How many customers opt into your offers of promotional and service e-mail lists

• *Opt out.* How many customers request to be taken off your e-mail lists

• *Carryover customers.* The number of preexisting customers who buy from your site as well as from your physical locations, catalogs, and direct sales

• *Monthly orders.* Orders month to month, except expected seasonal jumps, particularly Christmas

• *Annual orders.* Orders year to year (For example, when you compare one holiday season to the prior one, or one spring to the prior one, seasonal buying patterns are minimized and you can measure your progress for key buying periods.)

• *Inventory turns.* What items sell quickly through the site and what do not, as recorded by inventory tracking software

• *Returns.* What items are being returned. Poor retain patterns can signal a disconnect or deficiency between your ordering system, customer support, and customer expectations. Review returns closely to see where you need to add product descriptions, add or clarify internal site links, have service reps introduce themselves through pop-up screens, or add other tools that will help customers fully understand the product and its benefits before they order.

Reporting results. Just about all e-commerce and customer support systems include reports that track results. Your Webmaster will be able to tell you which reports from your site's server logs are already set up to report the information you want to track. Access logs available from your Internet service simply tell you how many hits each page is receiving, i.e., how frequently each page is accessed by Web site visitors. Using access logs, you can track where visitors have traveled and determine if some pages that you thought would be popular are, in fact, being ignored by visitors. By tracing commonly taken paths through the site, you'll be able to tell if customers are finding the information you've put there for them.

Michael Fischler, principal of The Pubs Group, a Web consulting firm in Los Angeles, frequently consults on customer service issues and recommends that, instead of trying to decipher server logs on their own, small-business owners use software reporting tools that scoop up the logs and create reports from them. WebTrends's Log Analyzer and Accrue Software's Hit List are both inexpensive packages that track the server logs and translate the results into plain-English reports.

The code that directs an e-mail to you from your Web site also can contain clues as to what point—i.e., on which page—customers realize they need extra help. This e-mail was sent to Fischler from his own Web site, from the "tactical marketing" page:

TIP The simplest formula for measuring return on investment (ROI) is to first create a baseline for comparison—say, the percent of customers who respond to e-mailed special offers. Then, track the expenses associated with adding in a particular customer support technology, such as instant chat. After the customers have been helped via the new technology for a month, review the number of sales per site visitor, compared to the number of sales per site visitor prior to the addition of the technology. Divide the incremental increase in the number of sales by the cost of the new technology to determine if the technology is beginning to pay off.

One caveat: Other factors will also affect sales—discounted prices, addition of new products, and advertising campaigns. Precise tracking of ROI in new customer service technologies requires a specific, concerted effort.

Date: Thu, 16 Nov. 2000 06:30:30 -0700 (PDT)
From: nobody@lainet.com
To: mrf@pubsgroup.com
Subject: Automatic email generated by form
The following was generated by the form located at
* http://www.pubsgroup.com/tactical_marketing.htm
(Note: The URL at the end is the address of the page the user was viewing when he decided to send the e-mail.)

Server logs themselves do not record when an e-mail was sent from a Web site—unless that e-mail is in a structured form with boxes for customers to fill out with their name, address, etc., that occupies its own Web page. In that case, the activity of the e-mail page, itself, is recorded (i.e., how often customers landed on the page that contains an e-mail form). E-mails generated by a generic pop-up box are much more customer-friendly than structured forms, Fischler explains, but then the burden is on you to keep track of the specific pages customers were viewing when they created the e-mail. This is a separate tracking process from analyzing the server logs.

Measuring ROI. When it comes to determining your return on investment (ROI) for specific customer service tools, such as online chat, consider, for example, the cost per chat and "buy" rate. Lance Rosenzweig, CEO and co-founder of PeopleSupport.com, an outsourcing company that provides live online chat and customer service reps to do the chatting, says that chat sessions vary in cost but tend to run about $4 to $5—about the same as a customer-service phone call. Yet the astounding results of live chat eclipse the cost. Normally, only 1.5% to 2% of visitors to any e-commerce site actually buy. PeopleSupport's studies indicate that up to 37% of customers who are able to immediately connect with customer service reps via online chat actually buy. Rapid response to customer queries via e-mail alone boosts the pur-

> **TIP** As you choose a system or expand your reliance on it, be sure to find out what reports and tracking services it offers. Do the reports tell you about buyer behavior, repeat purchasing, and customers' questions—as well as identify trouble spots on your site that are confusing to customers? And as you set up new programs, such as opt-in e-mail lists, be sure to include a way to track results from the very beginning. That way, you won't have to retrace your steps to establish a baseline after the program has been operating. It also makes sense to draw your accounting, shipping, and inventory managers into the process of selecting or improving your online CRM tools. These people will be the first to notice, for example, an unusually high proportion of returns from orders generated on a certain day, or that the label-printing software tends to crash under high volume, delaying shipping.

chase rate to 30%, and a toll-free customer assistance phone number lifts the buy rate to 20%, according to PeopleSupport, which offers all those options.

Once you've established a level of trust with your customers, you can add more personal service. Have your customer service reps record the questions that customers frequently ask, including those regarding products, services, and online functions that they wish your site offered. Customers who have ordered several times may appreciate an option to store their credit-card number and ordering information at your site to create their own "express lane" when ordering.

eHobbies.com, which provides information and goods to people devoted to birdwatching, collecting trains, and other pastimes, found that site visitors were becoming frustrated when they couldn't get additional information about arcane products immediately—and they expressed that frustration when they called or e-mailed. eHobbies's managers figured that if they came up with a way to keep customers on the site longer and satisfy their curiosity, they'd have a greater chance of selling to them. They were right.

Once eHobbies introduced online chat in April 2000, it found out that 75% of customers who used the 24-hour service were intensely interested in buying products; they just needed a little extra information to make up their minds.

Use reports for forecasting. Reports can tell you more than just what has happened; you can also use them to forecast demand for customer service. When you start with e-commerce, you'll be estimating demand for certain items, the quantity and complexity of customer inquiries, and other service functions. As you ramp up your e-commerce capabilities, you can use feedback, not estimates, to have an adequate number of service reps on hand at peak times and to make sure you have sufficient inventory and shipping supplies to get orders out.

Graphic artist Rebecca Collins, of Dallas, runs a custom pet portrait service called Art Paw. Customers send her photos of their pets and she scans them into her computer and inserts the pets' pictures into digitized versions of classic artworks and styles of art, such as Leonardo de Vinci's *Mona Lisa* and Andy Warhol-style pop art. Collins communicates with customers via e-mail to help them decide what artistic style they prefer before they place the order, so she can make sure that she has, for example, enough specialized paper, in the right sizes, on hand to accommodate the orders quickly. She also tracks customers' interests in various art genres so she can find additional digitized classic artworks to offer as demand rises for a particular genre.

People tend to shop further ahead when purchasing through a Web site than when shopping at a local store or through a mail-order catalog with which they've had a prior positive experience. The surge for online

Christmas shopping, for example, appears to begin the week before Thanksgiving and peaks about the 15th of December, declining after that, according to Marc Daniels, vice president of UGOdirect.com, a division of UGO Networks, a New York online game retailer (see "Mouse-to-House Time," on page 86). If you're an online retailer highlighting the ability to accept orders right up to, say, noon on December 24th, be sure to say so—and be doubly sure that you can fulfill those orders.

Customers genuinely appreciate the chance to give feedback about what's easy, hard, smart, and dumb about your e-commerce operation. E-LOAN, a company that provides online applications for consumer and business loans, has set a company policy that a human answers the customer service phone within six seconds. Its goal is for 90% of its e-mails to be answered within two hours, and 100% within 24 hours. Follow-up surveys with E-LOAN customers about quality of service indicate that 95% use E-LOAN again—an extremely high repeat rate by any standard.

TIP Try a trial run. Consider setting up a customer advisory board to test out new site features, offers, customer service technologies, and changes in your fulfillment operation. If your customers are geographically close to you, they may be happy to troop into your location and take a spin through demonstrations of the various technologies before you post them live on the site. (And, of course, they'll be more motivated to give their advice if you offer complimentary gift certificates or other types of compensation.)

Another option: Set up a "dummy" Web site that is password protected, and invite your consumer advisory board to prod and poke it for ordering and customer service glitches.

Tracking

MOUSE-TO-HOUSE TIME

Few merchants have customers that are as impatient as Marc Daniels's customers. He's vice president of UGOdirect.com, a division of UGO Networks, an online retailer of trendy electronic games, in New York City. Hard-core gamers line up to be the first to get their hands on the games that UGO sells. When they want them, they want them *now*. Daniels's challenge is to make sure that the games are shipped within moments of confirmation of payment. If they aren't, UGOdirect's fickle customers will run to another Web site or offline store that claims to be able to get them their games.

When UGOdirect first went online, Daniels examined every step of its existing customer service and fulfillment operation. He held customer focus groups, sent out questionnaires to random sets of customers, and held lengthy conversations with individual customers. "I asked them, is the service that we provide greater than going to the local store?" he recalls. "It really gets down to mouse-to-house time—the time that elapses from when the customer clicks the mouse (to send the order) to when it arrives at his house. It has to be a better experience than he can get in the local retail environment. If the order is placed today, it has to be shipped today."

That level of urgency persuaded Daniels that outsourcing fulfillment to a third-party warehouse was not the way to go. The warehouse would be unlikely to care as much as UGOdirect would about getting games out the door. So, the company does its own fulfillment, and Daniels has taken a continuous-improvement approach to customer service: He's constantly looking for ways to make it faster and better.

First, Daniels made sure that his Web site was fully supported by customer service reps. But soon, the company's 24 reps were unable to uphold the company's policy that no caller should be on hold for more than one minute. So Daniels signed on an outsourced call center to handle the overflow at peak times. The outsourced center is in Kansas City, but callers don't know that. The next caller is simply forwarded to the next service rep, no matter where he or she is located.

Next, Daniels took advantage of two customer service packages. One was eGain, an e-mail management package that helps group and respond to e-mails in a timely fashion. The other was eShare, a live chat function, that lets service reps carry on a text conversation with a customer who's currently at the Web site. Though he's expecting to add voice-over-Internet capabilities, Daniels says that the phone support and live chat—backed up by the outsourced call center—are keeping pace with the demands of the customer calls and 1,000 orders that UGOdirect fields daily. To monitor the operations, the supervisor of each customer service function generates weekly reports on the number of customers served, how quickly, and how many customer interactions resulted in sales.

In fall 1999, with Christmas fast approaching, Daniels turned his attention to fulfillment and shipping. It was taking as long as a day for an order to go from the Web site to being shipped. He chose a software system from FASCOR that cut the time from order acceptance to packing and labeling to five minutes. Once a customer hits "Submit," the order is forwarded to a wireless in-house system that directs the next available packer to start working on it. "All the convenience of online ordering goes right out the door if the product doesn't get to its destination in a timely fashion," concludes Daniels.

Tracking

Re-invest savings in technology. As more people become comfortable dealing online with businesses, you will be able to shift a greater proportion of your customer service and communications to Internet-based tools. As you do, track the amount of money you are spending on offline customer support functions to see how much you are saving. You may be able to divert money freed by reduced offline functions to improve and upgrade technology for online customer support.

Dr. Gregory Pecchia, a doctor who practices in Orange County, Calif., found that his staff became 20% more efficient and that his actual operating costs decreased after he subscribed to an online practice management service operated by Alteer, an application service provider. The software component of the service includes an e-mail feature that enables physicians to communicate with patients, answering questions, scheduling appointments, and transmitting certain test results.

The cost of the subscription to Alteer is $250 per month per doctor. Pecchia's office upgraded its computers to accommodate the greater volume of e-mails and expanded amount of data in electronic files, at a leasing cost of $250 per month. A high-speed DSL line costs only $120 a month. The total annual costs to Pecchia's practice of about $7,000 produced a documented savings of $30,000, while its overhead costs have dropped from the industry average of 60% of revenues to 50%.

Proactive customer service. Customer service should not only be reactive. Ask customers what they'd like to tell you. Follow up online sales with an e-mail to welcome customers. Include an interactive survey inviting them to tell you how you can make their lives easier. Offer options such as automatic renewal of consumables (such as office supplies or fresh flowers) or a reminder service to reschedule services (such as window washing or car maintenance).

You can also post a feedback form on your Web site that enables customers to make comments, complaints, and suggestions online. Assign one staffer to collect the feedback, respond to customers, and follow up internally. When you make changes in response to their comments, let your customers know by sending them e-mails and highlighting the improvements on your site.

Customers who have shopped at your site only once may also yield some valuable insights. Follow up a week or two after their order is fulfilled to see what they consider to be the strengths and weaknesses of your e-commerce site, especially compared to your competitors' sites. They may say, for example, that your minimum shipping charge is too high, or that they never got a response when they e-mailed your customer service reps with a question about assembly. And, be sure to follow up their response with a thank-you gift certificate or discount.

Analyze online vs. offline consumers. As you build profiles of your typical online buyers, compare them to your offline customers. Online customers may prefer merchandise that's more (or less) expensive than your offline buyers prefer. They may have more, or less, tolerance for substitutions and other common ordering complications. They may order in larger quantities to consolidate shipping charges and thus reorder less frequently. They may be more willing to experiment with new products than your offline customers. Such information is invaluable when you are planning expansions of your online services. You'll get the most return from new services that are most appealing to the broadest number of customers.

Once you have a well-established base of online customers, you can benchmark their buying habits and project the amount of money you can profitably spend to enrich your company's site, add more inventory, and adjust factors such as the cost of shipping.

The quality of customer service directly impacts your company's reputation. You may want to assign an employee to regularly check chat sessions, message boards, and listservs outside your Web site that are frequented by your regular customers to see what kinds of comments are made about your products and level of service. Also check out BizRate.com, Epinions, Better Business Bureau Online, any online service ranking offered by your local chamber of commerce, and even your state attorney general's office to be sure that an unhappy customer hasn't lodged a complaint.

Capitalizing on the gains. Recent studies of the buying habits of online shoppers show that customer loyalty is a crucial factor in profitability, even more so than for offline companies. As retailers, service companies, and professional firms in particular, experiment with more ways to serve their customers through the Internet, they will discover precisely what sort of service brings customers back.

Based on their own frustrating experiences with Internet shopping, the founders of CarePackages.com decided at the outset to include avenues for immediate response to customer inquiries, says principal and co-founder Michael Moran. The Fairfield, Conn., firm provides "theme-ready" and "build-your-own" customized "care packages" of specialty foods, small gifts, and cards that can be sent to college students and children away at camp.

"As a startup, we didn't do traditional offline benchmarking," says Moran. Yet, the partners knew good customer service when they saw it. When CarePackages.com went live, its service reps concentrated on answering customers' e-mailed questions within an hour. Three months later, Moran added a toll-free phone number prominently displayed at critical points on the site—especially during the checkout process.

"Absolutely, more people buy when they call," he says. In fact, 95% of all callers end up completing the sale either through one of the company's 12 service reps directly, or online while also on the phone with the rep. Overall, 8% of the daily visitors to CarePackages.com make a purchase, with that rate jumping to 14% during special holiday promotions, such as Halloween and Valentine's Day. The rate would be much lower without the call center, contends Moran.

Now in its second year, CarePackages.com is reaping the benefits of its quick response to customer questions: About 40% of sales are to repeat customers. That's the kind of response that Moran was hoping to develop. "Good service yields repeat customers," he says. ■

COMPANIES AND SITES IN THIS CHAPTER

Accrue Software **www.accrue.com**

Alteer **www.alteer.com**

Art Paw **www.artpaw.com**

Better Business Bureau Online **www.bbb.com**

BizRate **www.bizrate.com**

CarePackages.com **www.carepackages.com**

Direct Marketing Association **www.dma.org**

eGain Communications **www.egain.com**

eHobbies.com **www.ehobbies.com**

E-LOAN **www.eloan.com**

Epinions.com **www.epinions.com**

FASCOR **www.fascor.com**

The Pubs Group **www.pubsgroup.com**

UGO Networks **www.ugo.com**

WebTrends **www.webtrends.com**

Tracking

CRM TECHNOLOGY MATRIX

This chart shows what hardware and software you need to implement specific functions of online customer relationship management. It assumes that you already have a server-based computer network and fast Internet access (DSL or faster).

CRM Application	Volume	Hardware Requirements	Software Specs	Outsourcing Possibilities
E-mail and mailing list (simple e-mail accounts and mailing lists)	300 names	Desktop PC, 300mhz Pent. II, 64MB RAM	Personal Information Management software	ISP with LDAP or other directory service
	10,000 names	Server, 500mhz Pentium III*, OS**, 128MB RAM, 384+ kbps DSL	Dedicated e-mail/directory server (Sendmail, Exchange, Notes)	ISP offering list management services and directory support
	50,000 names	Server, 750mhz/SMP Pentium III*, OS**, 256MB RAM, SCSI I/O subsystem, T1	Dedicated e-mail/directory server (Sendmail, Exchange, Notes)	High bandwidth service providers w/ LDAP capabilities
E-mail and mailing list (with customized messages fields and database back end)	300 names, limited variation between messages	Desktop PC, 450mhz Pentium II, 64MB RAM	Office software, including DB support and scripting capability	ISP or marketing firm
	10,000 names, medium variation, including database-driven targeted marketing	Server, 750MHz Pentium III*, OS**, 256MB RAM, T1	SQL back-end database, high capacity e-mail server	High bandwidth ISP, offering list management services and directory support
	50,000 names, high variation, including graphics and database elements	Server, 750MHz SMP Pentium III*, OS**, 512MB RAM, SCSI I/O, T1	SQL back-end database, high-capacity e-mail server	High bandwidth ISP (best kept in-house for management purposes)
Database for in-house customer support (used for help desk)	300 customers	Desktop PC, 500mhz Pentium III, 128MB RAM	Office database software with multi-user capabilities	Data management firm, customer support center
	5,000+ customers	Server, 750MHz Pentium III*, OS**, 256MB RAM, T1	SQL database back end with custom front end	Data management firm, customer support center

Category	Requirement/capacity	Hardware	Software	ISP/handling
Customer support Web site (enables customers to find products, etc.)	Static HTML pages, no dynamic content. 500,000 hits/mo. or less	Server, 500mhz Pentium III*, OS**, 128MB RAM, 768kbps DSL	Basic Web server software (Apache, IIS)	ISP
	Mostly static HTML, some database-driven pages, 500,000 hits/mo. or less	Server, 500MHz Pentium III*, OS**, 128MB RAM, 768kbps DSL	Basic Web server (Apache, IIS) with embedded scripting language and SQL back end	ISP with database hosting and programming services
	Dynamic, media-rich Web site with database-driven pages and secure e-commerce; 1 million hits/mo. or more	Server, 750mhz SMP Pentium III/Xeon* OS**, 512MB RAM, T1+	Customized application server back end (WebObjects, Notes, Oracle 8i)	High bandwidth ISP
Customer support center with e-mail and instant-messaging/chat capacity	5 service reps	Server, 500mhz Pentium III*, OS**, 128MB RAM, 384+ kbps DSL	Component software system using standard e-mail servers and applications	Best handled in-house using readily available software components
	25+ service reps	Server, 750mhz Pentium III*, OS**, 256MB RAM, T1	Customized support-desk application (Java) and standard e-mail back ends	Best handled in-house with outsourced programming of chat/messaging
Inventory management	25 items shipped/week	Desktop PC, Pentium II 450, 64MB RAM	Office database software	Best handled in-house
	26 to 100 items shipped/week	Desktop PC, Pentium III 500, 128 MB RAM	Dedicated inventory management/POS system	Best handled in-house
	101+ items shipped/week	Server, 750mhz Pentium III*, OS**, 256MB RAM, T1	Customized inventory system with multi-user support	Can be outsourced, but best managed in-house

* or comparable Power PO/Sparc ** Mac OS X, Linux, or NT
Source: John Ray, director of IT services, Blue Cosmos Design (www.bcdinc.com)

• CyberSpeak •

Application service provider (ASP) An Internet-based service that provides software or services that businesses can rent and use online.

Chat room A "space" created on the computer screen—usually, a pop-up box—that provides the setting for a conversation; for example, between a customer and a service rep.

Click-through rate The percentage of Web users who click on a link embedded in an e-mail or located at strategic points on a company's site to arrive at a Web page that the company wants them to see.

Cookie A small piece of code implanted on your customer's hard drive by your computer, which enables your site to recognize that customer when he or she returns to your site.

Database A repository of information about your customers, sales contacts, products, and other critical information, saved in large computer files in such a way that you can search and manipulate them for specific information.

Embedded links URLs included in Web sites or in the text of e-mail messages that link to other sites or pages.

Frequently asked questions (FAQ) A user-friendly format for answering questions via the Web site that usually are addressed to a company's receptionist or customer service reps.

Filters Subcategories in an e-mail management program that automatically sort e-mail into files and subcategories—or even automatically delete e-mail from some sources.

Firewall Hardware or software that is placed on the periphery of an organization's computer network. All traffic going into the internal network from the Internet is screened by the firewall to prevent any unauthorized users from entering or from accessing protected information.

Instant messaging (IM) Technology that allows users to send typed messages to each other in real time while both are online. To communicate, users must have the same IM software, such as ICQ or AIM.

Landing page A page on a Web site created explicitly to give a visitor more information about an offer promoted elsewhere in the site or in a promotional e-mail.

Netiquette Online etiquette, especially important for customer service reps who are writing e-mails and live chat messages.

Opt-in An Internet user's active choice to be put on an e-mail list. The choice is usually made by filling out a form or clicking a button on a Web site that says, for example, "please sign me up for notices about future offers."

Opt-out An Internet user's active request to be deleted from an e-mail list database on which he/she has automatically been placed. The fact that the user doesn't check a box indicating "please don't send me notices about future offers" is considered tacit permission to send him/her e-mail.

Page pushing When a customer service rep forces a particular Web-site page to pop up on a customer's screen, at the customer's request.

Real time At hand, present time. Online chat that pops up in a box so that customers and customer service reps can exchange comments is a "real-time" service. Answering customers' e-mailed questions, even as soon as 10 minutes later, is not "real-time" service.

Rich e-mail An e-mail message formatted to include animations, music clips, full-color graphics, and other attention-grabbing devices.

Stickiness Site functions and features that tacitly urge consumers to come back over and over again.

Viral marketing The process of encouraging readers to pass along an e-mail, your site's address, or other bit of information about your site, in the hopes that they'll tell their friends, who will tell their friends, in an exponential chain.

Voice over Internet software that enables customer service reps and customers to talk through the Internet and their respective computers' sound cards and speakers, while simultaneously remaining online on the company Web site.

ONLINE CRM RESOURCES

These hardware, software, and service companies offer customer service and relationship management tools. Visit their Web sites for information on specific products, services, and prices.

CRM SOFTWARE

CertifiedMail.com **www.certifiedmail.com**

Commtouch **www.commtouch.com**

Delano Technology **www.delanotech.com**

Descartes Systems Group **www.descartes.com**

epicRealm **www.epicrealm.com**

iQ.com **www.iq.com**

ITXC **www.itxc.com**

Microsoft's ListBot **www.listbot.com**

MyOrders **www.myorders.com**

Nuasis **www.nuasis.com**

QuestivA **www.questiva.com**

RightNow Technologies
www.rightnowtech.com

Sand Hill Systems
www.sandhillsystems.com

vCustomer **www.vcustomer.com**

Vignette **www.vignette.com**

E-MAIL LIST MANAGEMENT SOFTWARE AND SERVICES

e2 Communications **www.e2software.com**

List-Universe.com **www.list-universe.com**

SparkLIST **www.sparklist.com**

E-MAIL INTEREST GROUPS

eGroups.com **www.egroups.com**

EzineCentral.com **www.ezinecentral.com**

EzineSeek.com **www.ezineseek.com**

Ezine-Universe.com **www.ezine-universe.com**

Newlettersforfree.com
www.newslettersforfree.com

BACK OFFICE AND FULFILLMENT

Date-Certain.com **www.date-certain.com**

FASCOR **www.fascor.com**

iFulfill.com **www.ifulfill.com**

iLink Global **www.ilinkglobal.com**

ReturnView **www.returnview.com**

SmartShip.com **www.smartship.com**

Stamps.com **www.stamps.com**

The Return Exchange **www.returnexchange.com**

FEEDBACK AND TRACKING SOFTWARE AND SERVICES

Buystream.com **www.buystream.com**

Envive **www.envive.com**

Informative **www.informative.com**

SatMetrix **www.satmetrix.com**